Short Berry Cake

SHORT BERRY CAKE

*A Memoir of One Village
& One Family in Vermont
Before World War II*

by **Polly Simmons Williams**

Published by Book Surge, LLC
An Amazon.com Company

© 2005 Polly S. Williams
All Rights Reserved

ISBN 1-4196-0762-6 (hard cover)
1-4196-0761-8 (soft cover)

DEDICATION

To my brother, Frederick Simmons, 1927-2004.

With love, Polly

SHORT BERRY CAKE

SHORT BERRY CAKE

TABLE OF CONTENTS
& List of Photographs

PROLOGUE _____ 1
Hand-drawn Map of Simmons Homestead _____ 2

CHAPTER 1: Simmons Family History _____ 3
George W. & Abigail Simmons _____ 4
Geo. H. Simmons Lamp Filler _____ 7
Abigail Simmons & Baby H.C. _____ 8
H.C. Simmons as Artist _____ 9
Three Views of the Tinshop _____ 11-12

CHAPTER 2: The Village _____ 13
Upper Main Street _____ 13
Paran Creek Falls _____ 15
The Marble Sidewalks on Main Street ____ 16
North Bennington Fire Department _____ 17
North Bennington Station _____ 19
Lincoln Square _____ 21
Early Refrigerator _____ 22
"Come as a Baby" Party _____ 23
Frederick M. Simmons _____ 24
The Model T _____ 25
On the Tobin "Side Lawn" _____ 26
Upper Main Street & "Cutter" _____ 28
"Here Comes Patricia!" _____ 30

CHAPTER 3: The Early Days _____ 31
Mother & Daddy _____ 31
Sailor Twins _____ 32
The Family Homestead _____ 33
Birthday Party at Jolivettes _____ 34
The Four of Us _____ 35
Our Icehouse & Storehouse _____ 36
Storehouse & Foundry _____ 38

iii

CHAPTER 4: Nanny ___ 39
Nanny ___ 39
Richmond & Mary Galusha ___ 40
Galusha Family ___ 41
The Simmons Brothers ___ 42
Clayton Gibson ___ 43

CHAPTER 5: Muckross ___ 45
Muckross ___ 45
Mother in the Flowers ___ 46
Muckross Trolley Shelter ___ 46
Polly at Muckross ___ 47
The Cabin at Muckross ___ 48
Letter to Santa ___ 50

CHAPTER 6: Winter and the Holidays ___ 51
Winter Picnic ___ 52
Skiing ___ 52
Family Christmas ___ 53
Maggie & Mary Sheldon ___ 54

CHAPTER 7: School Days ___ 57
Old Post Office & Bank ___ 57
Dance Recital ___ 60
Ice Cream Freezer ___ 62

CHAPTER 8: Weekly Schedule ___ 63
Halloween ___ 66

CHAPTER 9: The Depression ___ 67

CHAPTER 10: Summer & Short Berry Cake ___ 77
Our Flag ___ 79
Mother and Daddy on Memorial Day ___ 81
Girl Scouts & Wildflowers ___ 82
Calvin Coolidge Handshake ___ 84

Bud-Dog & Kids _____ 89
Reading the Sunday Paper _____ 90
Polly & Bud-Dog _____ 91
"Fregit" and "Hyatt" _____ 92
H.C. Simmons & Sons _____ 94
Miss Marian and Girl Scouts _____ 95
In Front of Library _____ 96

CHAPTER 11: Teenage Years _____ 97
Teenage Friends _____ 98
Sixteen _____ 100

CHAPTER 12: Summer of '39 _____ 101
Two of the "Worldly Ones" _____ 102
Junior Prom 1941 _____ 104

CHAPTER 13: War _____ 105
Richie Fonteneau's B-24 _____ 106

Acknowledgements _____ 109

SHORT BERRY CAKE

PROLOGUE

Several years ago, my granddaughter, Kirsten, gave me a book called *Legacy*—a sort of workbook for a life history—and with it was the admonition to "start writing." Consequently, I have been thinking and reminiscing and reliving those eighty years in my mind. It seems impossible that so many years have gone by.

Driving down "Meadow Lane" in Dorset recently, I thought, *Am I really the same person who, fifty years ago, walked down this road for dinner every night at the Barrows House—with two little girls scrubbed and dressed in their best?* It is truly hard for me to relate to that young woman, but it really was me—just in another time and place.

There have been three "me's." My first "time and place" was in North Bennington, Vermont, from my birth until I was nineteen. That's where I will start this epistle. My grandmother, Nanny, wrote a diary all of her life. I have backed up my recollections with excerpts from that diary, written as the events happened. To all of my family and friends who may remember a different version, I apologize, but this is the way I remember it.

SHORT BERRY CAKE

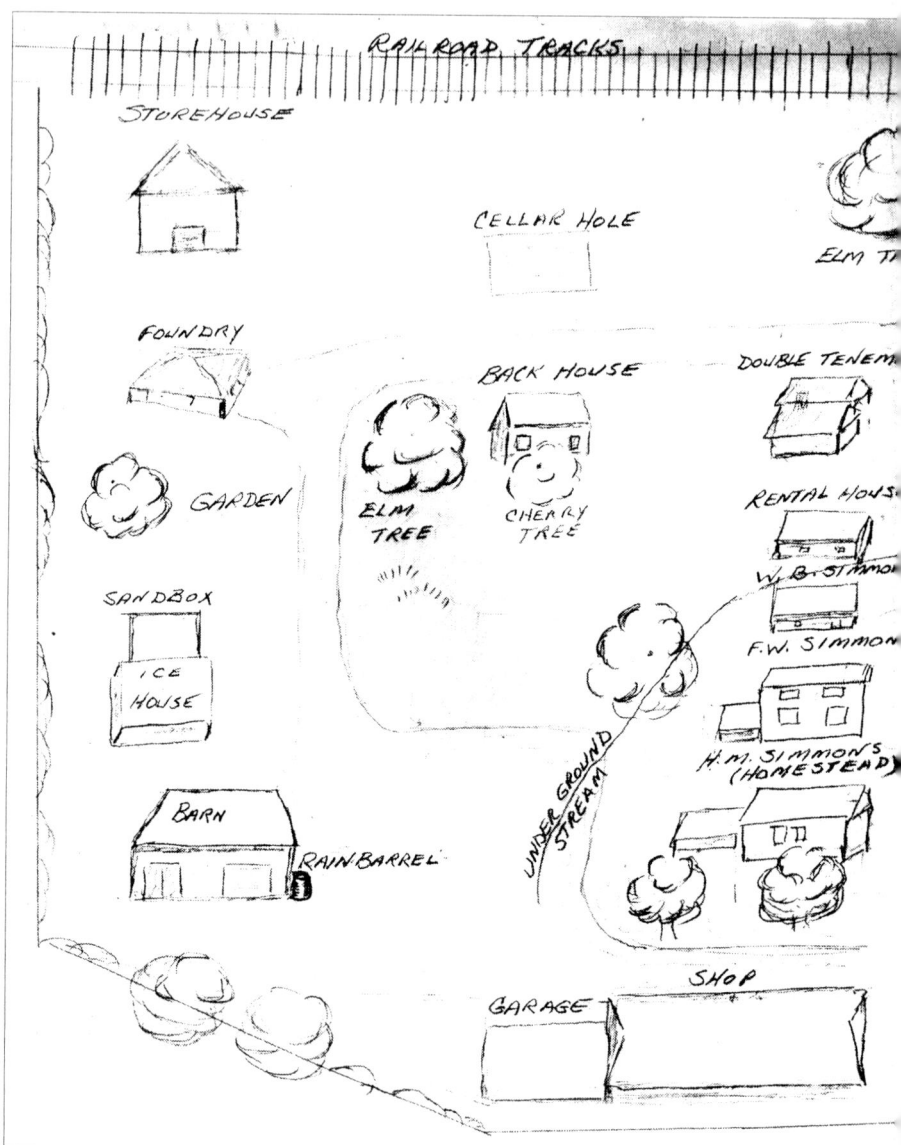

Hand-drawn map of Simmons Homestead—Polly Simmons Williams

CHAPTER 1

Simmons Family History

We came from interesting people. This first chapter traces the earliest recollections of my father's family beginning with my great-grandfather, George W. Simmons. He was born in New York State on January 22, 1803, the year that Lewis and Clark started their great adventure opening the West. The western boundary of the United States was the Mississippi River, and Thomas Jefferson was president.

George W.'s father, also named George, was a merchant seaman and "went down with his ship" in 1805 at the age of 50. We don't know what happened to their mother, Laura, but the children, George W., about two years old, and his sister, Maria, five, were sent to their guardians in Charleston, South Carolina. Maria went to live with family friends, William and Maryann McCready. Maryann had a hat shop at 209 King Street in Charleston. William, like his friend George, was a merchant seaman and also died at sea in 1817. The court-appointed guardian of George W. was Henry A. deSaussure, a young lawyer from a prominent South Carolina family.

According to letters from deSaussure, George W. learned to read and write, and eventually was apprenticed to a tinsmith to learn the trade. We know very little of his years in Charleston except that he was devoted to his guardian and ultimately named his first son in his honor. In 1818, he received a leather-bound Bible from the Charleston Bible Society. Inside the front cover is his name written in script and spelled "Simons" and in pencil above is written "Simmons." Inside the back cover is a rough sketch of a schooner.

When he was about 19, he left Charleston and the deSaussure family, taking his tinsmithing tools with him. Why he left

Charleston, we do not know, but according to letters from the McCready family, his departure was sudden and secret. It was about 10 years before he tried to make contact with his remaining family in South Carolina. From stories in the family, we surmise he spent those years in New Orleans, Louisiana, and, eventually, at the age of 27, he headed north to New York and the Albany area where he was born.

George W. Simmons & Abigail Willis Simmons
Parents of my grandfather, H.C. Simmons

In 1830, he moved to Bennington, Vermont, and took the Freeman's oath, which permitted him to vote and to own property. By 1833, he had met and married Abigail Pettis Willis. Her brother, Abel, lived in Bennington, and her family came from Franklin, Connecticut. They named their first child George Henry for his father, George, and his guardian, Henry deSaussure. In 1835, George W. purchased land in East Bennington Village near the Norton Pottery Factory. He built a shop and gained a reputation as a fine metal worker.

SHORT BERRY CAKE

George's business was growing, and so was his family—he needed more space. So, in 1850, he came to North Bennington and rented 87 rods of land from Sidney Colvin. He was to pay $32.63 on each and every first of April for the term of a thousand years. They believed in long leases. I wonder if we still owe rent on the land!

He built a small shop there and, next to it, eventually built a fine house for his growing family. In 1857, Col. C.R. Merriam, a friend of the family, wrote to George W., "your family will have a very pretty house...when it is finished." More houses and outbuildings for the business were built on the land. A spring on the northwest corner of the property supplied water for all the buildings.

Though their business prospered, Abigail and George had much sadness in their lives. Two of their children, Frederick and Hiram died at birth, and James Lauren died at 3 months. The wonderful bubbling spring on the property must have been the culprit for the typhoid deaths of Maria, Mary McLean, and Alice in 1860 and 1861—they were all young women in their twenties. Ten years later, Maggie and Carrie died. The two surviving children were George Henry, born in 1834, and the youngest child, my grandfather Horatio Clayton, born in 1857. He was known as Clay or H.C.

On December 25, 1855, George Henry and Sara E. Coombs, whose father was the local druggist in North Bennington, were married. They lived with Sara's family in the cobblestone house across the street from the Simmons family.

The War Between the States was gaining momentum, and, in addition to the grief of losing his children, George W. searched for news of his sister, Maria, the McCreadys, the deSaussures, and other friends in the South. He was unable to locate any news of them. He died broken-hearted in 1863.

George Henry, though he lacked the artistic talent of his father, was an early day entrepreneur. As a child in Bennington, he begged his father to allow him to work in the mill as most of

SHORT BERRY CAKE

his friends did—their home was near the cotton mill, and George loved to spend his Saturdays "helping " his friends complete their work. His father was adamant, though, and said that when he commenced work at anything in particular, he had better "learn a trade of some kind."

Now, with the death of his father, George H. took over the running of the tinshop. He had grandiose ideas—but cash was needed. So, he approached his father-in-law, Hiram Coombs with plans for borrowing some capital.

This was the answer:

"Victory, Nov. 27, 1865

"Dear George—I think I have had the final talk with Father—he says there is a better way than to make such a debt now—he says he will let me have the money, but it is with his mind so much opposed to it that I am unwilling to take it. So, in listening to his talk and all others about the prospect of business matters, I have myself become fearful that it is too great a venture.----

"----I have a plan that would suit me better and I think be as well for you. It is to build up that new part in front and use it for your salesroom and when the time came, move your shop on the garden back of Houghton's store."

We don't know what George's idea was, but, obviously, Hiram turned it down. An interesting note though—George must have relented and Hiram's ideas were used in remodeling the shop. Today, the so-called salesroom has a second floor, and the old original shop is being used as a garage on the back part of the building, on what surely must have been "the garden back of Houghton's store."

After the Civil War, the tinsmith shop continued to grow—it now specialized in oil cans (one of G.H Simmons' inventions in 1858), and in parts for commercial weaving looms (using the expertise G.H. learned in the cotton mills of his youth), oil lamps, and, of course, the promotion of the many other Simmons inventions. But, as time went on, George became more and more interested in politics.

Flyer advertising one of George H.'s inventions

He was a Democrat and a recognized leader of his party in Vermont. He was elected a Justice of the Peace for many terms and was also town auditor. In 1874, he was elected Judge of Probate for Bennington. The *Vermont Gazette* in 1874 reported that when the last returns were counted the night of the election, the friends and neighbors of George H. Simmons conducted an impromptu celebration "with cheerful strains of music from our cornet band, bonfires burned brilliantly, and the church bells of the village were vigorously rung."

Abigail Simmons & baby H.C., my grandfather

In the meantime, Horatio Clayton, youngest son of George W., was learning to take over the shop of his father and brother, which was now called G.W. Simmons Sons.

Shortly after the inauguration of President Cleveland in 1885, George H. was rewarded for his many years of service to the public and his party by his appointment as a special agent of the Treasury Department. This was the forerunner of the Secret Service. He was assigned duty at the port of New York where he unearthed many long-practiced frauds against the Revenue Department in the import business.

So George H. left Vermont and turned over the running of the shop to his brother, H.C. Simmons. He died in 1892 after many successful years of work with the government. His wife Sara had preceded him in death 10 years earlier.

The artist, Horatio Clayton Simmons

H.C. was only 28—22 years younger than his brother George—and I imagine that he took the job with great reluctance. He was an artist of some distinction and an accomplished musician. He could play any stringed instrument could "triple tongue" on the cornet, and led a local band. A quotation by a local news reporter in 1887 upon returning to the village after many years gave an interesting slant on his character.

"...we captured our old friend and schoolmate, Horatio C. Simmons. His congenial nature soon renewed our acquaintance. We found him at home in his business and before we could get away from him; we were invited over to hear the sweet tones of his best violin. 'In this dull place music is all we have to animate us.'"

On March 15, 1888, H.C. Simmons and Martha Galusha were married at the Galusha home on Holy Smoke Road in Shaftsbury. They "set up housekeeping" in a small house on upper Main Street in North Bennington, but after the death of his sister Maggie Sheldon and mother Abigail, they moved to the homestead on Main Street. There, they raised 5 children: Carolyn, William Bernice, Herman McClean, Frederick Merriam, and Alice.

The shop business was flourishing, and H.C. continued the heritage of his father and brother by acquiring a patent in 1894 for an improved steam heating boiler, which ultimately was manufactured at the shop. Between 1894 and 1930, there were between six and seven thousand Simmons steam heaters throughout the eastern part of the United States.

The photographs on the following pages show the evolution of the business. Some of the same workers appear in later pictures. Who are they?

Continuing the family tradition, H.C.'s sons, Bernice, Herman (Jack) and Fred, worked in the business until they went off to war in 1914. In 1918, the boys were summoned home because of the sudden death of their father, Horatio Clayton Simmons. The company was now called H.C. Simmons Sons.

The creative heritage of the Simmons continued in 1932 with the invention by William Bernice of an early type of home fuel oil burner for a fluid fuel-burning furnace. In 1933, an additional patent was granted for an improved boiler to take advantage of the new oil burner—the nickel-plated demonstration model boiler can be seen at the Bennington Museum. The Simmons

SHORT BERRY CAKE

Above: Tinshop in 1884—notice the gas streetlight
Below: Winter 1898—there is H.C.'s ever-present derby hat
& the Simmons homestead next door

made many fine heating boilers, both oil and coal-fired. They were installed throughout the Northeast, and the last one was built at the time of World War II.

The world was changing. New technology created by the war and the uncertainty of the postwar years made this relatively small operation obsolete. In addition, the so-called "future crew"—the next generation of Simmons Sons—Arthur, Allen and Frederick—had been to college, gone off to another war, and had seen the world beyond the one where they grew up. Their generation was branching out and the world was a challenge. They wanted to move on, and, after more than 100 years of operation, the Simmons Tinshop closed its doors.

The newly remodeled shop in 1900

SHORT BERRY CAKE

CHAPTER 2

The Village

According to a recent town report, our village was originally called Haviland's Hamlet until 1776 when it was discovered that Mr. Haviland was a Tory. His son-in-law, Mr. Sage, made the exposure; the village promptly became Sages City, which it continued to be called until 1828, when a post office was established by the government. North Bennington, Vermont, as is has been called ever since, covers only 2.1 square miles. In 1923, it consisted of Main Street running north and south. This was a series of three hills and was about a mile long from Grandview cemetery (which actually was in Shaftsbury) to the

This is upper Main Street in the summer of 1923. That's Pete Panos leaning against his store. If you look carefully past the A&P store, you can see the striped pole of Jack Clark's Barber Shop.

library on lower Main Street and then continuing down to Water Street past W.H. White's Kiddy Kar Company to the town line in Hinsdaleville. Turning obliquely off of the main street were Greenwich Street (we called it Shoe Lane) and Hawkes Avenue; Depot, Bank and Houghton Streets; EZ Lane (now Sage Street); Prospect and West Street, Hillside Street, and the River Road. The east-west axis was the railroad line that ran through the northern edge of the village in upper Main Street.

This was many years before the days of shopping malls. In fact, the word "mall" only meant "a shaded walk in St. James Park, London," and we had never heard the word. But on both sides of "upper" and "lower" Main Street, we had shops to supply all our needs. On upper Main Street was a small park with a fountain commemorating all Veterans of World War I. Next to the park was Panos' ice cream store (and penny candy, too). Ed Simonds ran the A&P store next to Jack Clark's Barber Shop, and next to it was the Morrisey short-order restaurant that my mother called the Greasy Spoon. An alley separated these shops from the Simmons brick block, which was built by my grandfather in 1903 and held the new post office and Dick Dwyer's Meat Market. Apartments—or as we called them "tenements"—were on the second and third floors. The next building was a house built in 1948 by Warren Dutcher. It was built entirely of cobblestones, and Mr. Dutcher raffled it off, selling tickets at $1.00 each. Paul Shuffleton of Arlingtron held the winning ticket. I have often wondered how many tickets Mr. Dutcher sold. Across from the Simmons homestead, the next houses then were Dr. Tobin's, the W.R. White house, the Bake Shop, the Bake Shop house, and the railroad station.

On the opposite side of the street and across from the park were the bank and Meagher's Grocery Store (later to become Powers and Robinson), the only place open on Sunday nights, and the only place to buy a Bermuda onion. The Meagher homestead was next door and Stella "Somebody"—I think her name was Chevlin—ran a drug store for a few years. Next up the street was a gas station run by Jimmy Huntington (he also sold a vile new drink in a bottle called Moxie), and next to it was our shop, H.C. Simmons Sons, followed by the Simmons homestead where Nanny, Aunt Marcia and Uncle Jack lived. Next came our house and the "ell" next door, Aunt Mammie and Uncle Bernie's house, followed by our three tenement houses and the railroad tracks. In back of these houses was a house and barn that we rented to the Sinay family.

Paran Creek Falls

Lower Main Street was dominated by the millpond and falls of Paran Creek, which, in the early 1800s supplied water power for the mills located on its shores. This was the site also of the original town settled by Joseph Haviland, but the mills and many original buildings were washed away in a horrible flood in 1852. Now it was a docile stream with several falls that were bounded by partially abandoned buildings until it reached the falls at the thriving Cushman Company.

On this part of Main Street, our needs were supplied by Shepard's Store (now Powers Store), Marty Percey's newspaper store, and Jimmy Powers Dry Good Store, our brick McCullough library, and the McCullough fire station.

In walking to school or church, or really anywhere in North Bennington, we seldom used the sidewalks. A maze of footpaths going "crosslots" created the shortest paths to anywhere, and all kids and some adults used them. It was many years before I actually walked down Main Street on our beautiful marble sidewalks to go to school or the Congregational Church. Now I've noticed that the sidewalks have been torn up and replaced with concrete, and I wonder if the footpaths have survived.

Looking south on Main Street: notice our white marble sidewalks & the Bake Shop at far left.

For me, it was a longer walk down the hill to Shepard's Store, but I was always eager to go with Mother when we needed oysters. I was intrigued by the large metal tub on legs that stood outside the door. It held raw oysters (only in months with an R, of course) with no refrigeration. It was a 'serve-yourself' deal with a scoop to fill your cardboard carton. You just hoped the temperature wasn't too hot and the oysters weren't too old. Actually, no one worried about such things, and the oysters tasted much better than today.

In addition to these stores, we had Dewey Bronson's meat truck, which stopped at our door once a week with a great array of meat kept cool with chunks of ice. The rag and news-paperman, who must have been the original recycler, came once a

The volunteer firemen in 1914--ten years before I was born--but not much had changed in 1923! Left to right: Back row: Tom Nash, William Papus, Frank Welch, Art Barber, Jim Powers (Tom's father), Bernard Powers, Frank Powers (Chick), William Barber, Bob Burke, John Walsh, Walt Cole (my uncle). Front row: _____?, George White, Mike Howe, Buddy Powers, Willie Howe, George Campbell, Tom Lisbee, Al King, Jim Howe, Tom Mahar. In background, Tom Harlan (in derby hat).

SHORT BERRY CAKE

month. He paid us for old newspapers and rags or swapped for tin pans from his rickety old truck. Phoebe Bump and others peddled berries, produce, preserves, and horseradish all year. And we knew that spring was just around the corner when the scissors grinder with his pet monkey came to our door to sharpen our knives and scissors for the year.

George Mattison and his horse delivered our milk every morning. In the early years, we dipped the milk from a big can in the back of the wagon, but as things got more sophisticated, the milk was delivered in glass milk bottles. The washed empties were put out each night to be replaced by full bottles early in the morning. I don't suppose there was any sterilization of those bottles. There was no pasteurization or homogenization either; so thick, rich cream would rise to the top of the bottle. In the winter, it froze and popped up out of the bottle like a top hat. Licking it gave us an early version of ice cream. I still remember waking up to the sound of those clanking bottles as George went from door to door, and the unattended horse went clip-clopping down the street to the next corner.

Until 1927, we had excellent trolley car connections; we could hop on a trolley to go not only to Bennington and Hoosick Falls, New York, but also all the way to Northampton, Massachusetts. However, in that year spring floods wiped out all bridges and tracks and the whole service stopped running. It was the end of an era for most people, but for the Simmons boys, the empty trolley car barn became a great source of exploration. The brick car barn still stands at the intersection of Bank Street and the railroad tracks. After a few years, a bus line was established to Bennington, but it was no match for the trolley service as family cars gradually became the mode of transportation.

Halfway down Main Street from the cemetery was our bustling railroad station. Each day two passenger trains ran to New York and two to Montreal, so we could go to New York City, Montreal, Canada, and the "whole" world. In addition, there were "milk" trains (taking milk from the farms to the city each day except Sunday) and there were freight trains, "switchers," and shuttle trains to Bennington and Hoosick Junction. Fred Welling once said that there were sixteen passenger train movements each day. It was a pretty active place for a small village.

We could set our clocks by those trains. When we were swimming at the "Big Pond" in the late afternoon and heard the Green Mountain Flyer pulling into the station, we headed for home. It was four o'clock. Needless to say, the action around the station was a big part of our lives, and because of the proximity of our property, we knew them all—the engineers, the firemen, the porters, and the conductors. Sometimes the engineer would give us a ride up the tracks when they "switched" or filled the engine with water from the high water tower in the freight yard.

North Bennington Station

But mostly we just sat under the big elm tree that separated our property from the tracks and watched. There was something awesome and powerful about those engines. They belched cinders, smoke, a sulfur smell, and a lot of hissing steam and noise. There was always a small crowd of people watching the action as the trains rolled in. The conductor was first down the

SHORT BERRY CAKE

steps with his metal footstool for the ladies, whom he would help down one by one. Then, after the porters helped the departing passengers aboard, the stationmaster would ceremoniously look at the big watch that hung from a gold chain across his ample stomach. At his nod, the conductor shouted, "AHW...LLLL... ABOARD," and they would huff and puff and chug-chug-chug faster and faster away from the station on their way to a world that we could only imagine.

Back in the old days, business had been brisk and the village was thriving, so we had a splendid brick bank built in 1864 by Trenor Park. It held a large public hall on the second floor. In 1923, this was used for meetings and dances, and this was where we went to the movies on Saturday afternoon. Our movies were silent, except for the piano player, who played background music to embellish what was happening on the screen. Our neighbor Clara White played the piano, and sometimes I was allowed to sit on her bench, which was really close to the action. *Rin-Tin-Tin*, a big favorite, was a movie about a big German shepherd. I never tired of seeing him rescue a damsel in distress just in the nick of time as the pianist's hands raced up and down the keyboard. WOW! What excitement! And, of course, we rolled in the aisles over "Our Gang" or "The Little Rascals," as they are now called. The big kid in the series was Spanky McFarland. I treasured his autograph, which Aunt Carolyn sent to me when she visited in California.

Residential telephones were nonexistent and communication was by a note sent through the mail. In dire circumstances, we could use the telephone across the street at the Crawford Bakery. Then, of course, to contact people from out of town, we could use the telegraph at the railroad station. When I was about six years old, we had a telephone installed in our house, so our phone was the curiosity of the neighborhood and it never ceased to amaze everyone. Our number was "135 ring six." There were six people on our line, so we were supposed to pick up only when it rang six times. However, the sport of the day was

SHORT BERRY CAKE

Lincoln Square; Shepard's Store on left

SHORT BERRY CAKE

"listening in" on other conversations. I was cured quickly one day when I lifted the receiver ever so carefully to hear Edith McCarthy say, "Harriet Simmons, hang up that phone!" I thought the darned thing had eyes too.

When I was first born, Mother cooked on a kerosene stove, but about 1927 we bought a new electric one. However, Nanny kept her kerosene stove operating in her house because "you never know." When the flood of 1927 cut off all electricity for days, she was able to cook for us all. She predicted that these newfangled things would never last and we began to wonder. But before many years, we had an electric refrigerator. It was a General Electric with a big coil on top. There were no more blocks of ice and no more dripping ice pans, but how did it stay cold? Again, we were amazed.

Between 1920 and 1933, parties were prolific for our parents. This was the Roaring Twenties and the era of Prohibition. The government had forbidden the manufacture, transportation, and sale of intoxicating liquor. But, as with youth in all societies, defiance was the rule and how to beat the law was the goal. There were bootleggers and speakeasys and recipes for bathtub gin. Whether or not my family broke the law I do not know. I do know that they danced the Charleston, had costume parties, progressive dinners, and picnics. Any holiday was an excuse for a party, and Mother was the belle. She had wavy auburn hair, brown eyes, a bubbly personality, and she played the piano. Whenever she played "Let Me Call You Sweetheart," "My Sweetheart's the Man in the Moon," or any of the other hits of the era, people would gather around the piano and sing, some

SHORT BERRY CAKE

Is Mother pulling Uncle Bernie's hair?

1927: "Come as a Baby" party at our house. Back row, L to R: Wilbur Carroll, Jack Simmons, Carl Mattison, Poppy White. Middle Row: Chubby Simmons, Bernice Simmons, Marge Simmons, Mrs. Mattison, Marian White, Mrs. and Mr. Howe, Evelyn Payne. Front Row: Mad Simmons, Marcia Simmons, Wells White, Mrs. Carroll, Miss Payne, Nelson Payne.

accompanying with their ukuleles or kazoos. A kazoo was an instrument for non-musicians that amplified the sound of humming. Mother's favorite short party dress was made of pink chiffon covered from top to bottom with crystal beads. I'm certain Zelda never looked as great.

According to my Aunt Ellen, before meeting my father, my mother was engaged to a state trooper, who was very handsome. His name was Chester Johnson and he lived in Schenectady. But she met my father at a dance, they fell in love—and that was the end of Chester Johnson.

Frederick Merriam Simmons, my father

We didn't need a car, but we always had one for the three families, and we took turns using it a week at a time. For what? To go to Bennington on Saturday night to eat popcorn from Pop McGurn's wagon while we watched the people go by; for our many picnics; for going berry picking; getting to the Barnum and Bailey circus at Morgan's field in Bennington; and for Sunday drives to visit our many relatives.

We looked forward to these Sunday outings, which seemed to be spontaneous. Not many people had telephones, so our arrivals were not expected. However, the welcomes we received were genuine, the food was plentiful, and we loved seeing cousins and second cousins, aunts and great aunts up and down the county: the Galushas (Nanny's family) in Shaftsbury, the Squires (Mother's family) in East Arlington, the Remingtons (Mother's oldest sister) in Bennington, and the Sheldons (Simmons' in-laws) in Dorset.

Living in such close proximity, there must have been family feuds, but we were blissfully unaware of them. These things were best not disclosed to children, and I suspect my sweet, gentle grandmother ruled the family with an iron hand and would not tolerate dissension anyway. So we continued to grow up in LaLa Land, and it was lovely.

The Model T in back of Uncle Jack's porch (Tobin house in background).

For many years the only doctor in town was Dr. Tobin, who lived across the street from my grandmother. His office was in the front room in his house. There was no waiting room or nurse or any papers to be filled out. It really wasn't necessary because the doctor made house calls every day to check on you if you were ill. Otherwise, when you had an ache or pain, you just walked in. If he wasn't there, you wandered back in the house and usually found him slouched back in his easy chair, smoking a cigar and listening to a ball game on the radio.

His daughter Lucille, who was my friend, nicknamed him Bunny, which was what we all called him. As a special treat, he would take us with him when he made his rounds at the new Putnam Memorial Hospital in Bennington. My favorable impression of this wonderful new facility was based on the fact that Miss Baker, the revered supervisor of nurses, had a talking parrot.

Lucille and I spent many hours on her "side lawn" making houses with leaves. We raked leaves to make a floor plan, then made doll-sized furniture with burdock blossoms. The crowning touch was ten beautiful tiny Oriental rug samples loaned to us by Lucille's mother, Anna, whom I always called Auntie Tobin. We graduated from the leaf house to a room in the Tobin barn that we called the playhouse. I recall that we constantly cleaned the place with a broom, though we must have also "played house," which was the activity for little girls. One day, I was severely scolded for taking my father's "Flit" gun—the latest device for

Allen, "Hyatt," Lucille, & Art on the Tobin "side lawn."

SHORT BERRY CAKE

killing all insects—to get rid of the spiders in the playhouse. "Quick, Henry, the Flit" was a household slogan and seemed the logical answer to a playhouse insect problem as well. However, my parents did not share my point of view.

Aunt Millie (one of Mother's older sisters) and Uncle Walter Cole lived on Greenwich Street. This was one of the streets that lay within the town of Shaftsbury but was in the village of North Bennington. They had an acre of land, a house and small barn, a cow, several chickens, and a vegetable garden, but no indoor plumbing. The house was heated by a wood-burning parlor stove; all cooking was done on the big iron wood-burning range in the kitchen. Water was heated here, too. Sometimes Mother would take us up to their house when Aunt Millie made her butter in an old-fashioned churn. We would have hot toast with salty fresh "farmers'" butter and usually pickled pigs feet—it was so good!

One snowy winter day, my mother convinced Art Cole (Uncle Walter's brother who lived next door) to hitch up his horse to the cutter (a sleigh) and let Mother borrow it to drive my little brother and me around town. The roads were not salted in those days and the snow was hard-packed, so we had easy sleighing. It was so exciting to slide along with the bells on the horses' harnesses jingling, with the snow biting our cheeks, and to see the expression of confidence on our mother's face as she drove the horse. We tended to forget—if we ever knew—that Mother was born before the days of automobiles, and horses were the only means of transportation in her youth. Anyway, it was a memorable day and my last ride in a bona fide "cutter."

Mother's younger sister lived on Hall Street. It was a new street, mostly occupied by young families who were friends of our parents. It was a short walk from our house through the hedgerow in back of the shop, past Bud Norton's vegetable garden and the White apartment house, and across Bank Street; then, a short walk on the marble sidewalk, past Amy Surdam's beautiful tulip garden and across her new concrete driveway to a beaten path across an empty lot near the Vetelle house. I then crossed School Street near Sabina Howes' house. Walking the

SHORT BERRY CAKE

length of Hall Street in my memory, I can remember each family—Nora Stanley, our fifth and sixth grade fearsome but memorable teacher; the Willards; Crawfords; Paynes; Aunt Nee and Uncle Grange; the Whitmans. Across the street were the Jolivettes, Miss May Weir, and the Woods.

Upper Main Street, 1919—notice "cutter" & horse coming down the hill.

Mr. Wood, the principal of our school, lived across from Nora Stanley with his wife and daughter Patty. One day Mrs. Wood, hoping to impress the locals, gave a very formal luncheon party. It was impressive until teenager Patty served the lemon

SHORT BERRY CAKE

meringue pie. From the kitchen, Mrs. Wood's booming voice shouted, "Put the points toward them!" The Woods went on to greener pastures, but Mrs. Wood left me with a social grace that still haunts me whenever I serve pie.

For an era in which life was slow and easy—at least in retrospect—there was a compelling need in our town to shorten names or use nicknames. Obviously, this was not to save time, but seemed to be a better way of identification. Really, who would be caught calling Frederick Merriam Simmons, my father, by his full name? As a young boy, he was blond, a little plump, and rosy-cheeked, so he became Chubby. I can understand this, but then we had Gooly Powers, Dumpy Moxley, Jelly White, Hornet Simmons, Curly Fitzgerald, Stubby Green, Skunk Martin, Moe Salmon, Punk Sinay, Blossom Welch—the list is endless. How these names evolved we'll never know, but they stuck with their owners for the rest of their lives. I daresay that most people in the town didn't know the real name of Diddle Shanahan.

And so, this was the world that I was born into.

SHORT BERRY CAKE

News clipping—"Here comes Patricia!"
My mother and me

CHAPTER 2

The Early Days

March 22, 1923—Cold, snowy blizzard
Baby Harriet born 8:00 A.M. 7 ½ lbs.

—*Entry from Nanny's diary*

A raging blizzard was covering the roads with heavy snow that night when my father bundled Mother into the family 191- Model T Ford and headed for the hospital. I have been told it was a stressful five-mile trip at midnight, with Mother in labor and the car barely cutting through the huge drifts that had accumulated on the road. The relief must have been enormous when they finally climbed Bennington Hill and I was respectfully born under the roof of the new Putnam Memorial Hospital. It was March 22, 1923; my mother was twenty-two and my father was twenty-six.

Mother & Daddy

They named me Harriet Barber after my maternal grandmother, Harriet Barber Squires, who had died the year before. My mother always called me Polly, after the book Pollyanna, which was all the rage at the time. My cousins called me "Hyatt," which was their pronunciation of Harriet. For a reason that I can't fathom now, my name was always an embarrassment to me. I used to cringe on the first day of school when we had to announce our "real" names out loud.

Sailor Twins

SHORT BERRY CAKE

The September after my birth, Aunt Marcia and Uncle Jack, who lived with Nanny in the Simmons homestead next door, had twin boys, Arthur Clayton and Allen Nesbitt. I don't remember much about that year or the next couple of years, but I imagine the whole Simmons clan paid a great deal of attention to us.

We were the fifth generation to live on this property. My great-grandfather, George W. Simmons, had rented the property in 1854. My grandfather was born in the big house.

The Tinshop & the Family Houses

My earliest recollection is of being read to by Nanny. It was so comforting to snuggle down beside her in the rocking chair on her front porch and listen to her read the same books over and over. The books were from another era and had been read to her children. The Mother Goose book that was my favorite still has the torn corners that she used in doing "Fly away Jack, fly away Jill." Pieces of paper were stuck on the forefinger of each hand (Jack: left hand; Jill: right hand). "Fly away Jack"—put left hand

SHORT BERRY CAKE

behind head, tucking forefinger (with paper) under. "Come again Jack"—bring left hand out from behind head, and so on...

One night when my mother checked on me before she went to bed, I was missing from my room. After a great deal of commotion and searching of the neighborhood, they ultimately found me asleep in Nanny's rocking chair.

We were part of a large group of post-war babies and birthday parties became very competitive for our mothers. Little boys were dressed in sailor suits and little girls in ruffled dresses and Mary Jane patent leather shoes, which we shined with Vaseline. I especially remember the big beautiful hair ribbons that were the fashion. I coveted one that my friend, Lucille Tobin wore. Four inches wide and made of pink taffeta with cabbage roses, it was held on by gathering a hank of her hair with a rubber band and tying the ribbon over it.

Birthday Party at Jolivettes in 1927—(Marmie's socks always stayed up better than mine!) Left to right: Polly Simmons, Marjorie Jolivette, Ralph White, Betty Jane White, Charles White, Carnie White, Gerry Payne, Lucille Tobin, Art & Allen Simmons

The year I was four, my brother was born. He was named Frederick William, after my father and my Uncle Will. Things began to pick up after his arrival. At least, it seemed that way. He was just learning to creep one day when I lured him up the stairs, ever so slowly. I was thinking what a hero I would be if I coaxed him all the way up. Of course, he fell and I was banished.

The four of us—Polly, cousins Art & Allen, & Fred

So, now there were four of us, and it seemed that life centered on us. Because of the proximity of the business, my father, Uncle Jack and Uncle Bernie (he and Aunt Mammie lived in the house on the other side of us) were always available to teach us to "shout down the rain barrel" by the barn, take us to the pond to swim, or to referee any arguments. How lucky we were! They built us an oversized sandbox where the local toy manufacturers, W.H. White, had us test their latest inventions. The wooden kiddycars, steam shovels, and trucks had tough workouts by us before they ever hit the market. The alternative sandpile was the open shed in the barn—it was the sand used by the company to make cement. It was really off limits, but that made it seem bigger and better.

We had a big icehouse that held enough ice to supply all three families through the summer. Chunks about twelve inches square were cut in the winter on the big pond, brought down to our

SHORT BERRY CAKE

About 1930—Our icehouse above
The storehouse below; with Carnie White

icehouse and packed in sawdust. It was a great place to play after the ice melted down a bit and we could climb up high on the chunks. We always came home wet to the bone. Our wool leggings, jackets and mittens really soaked up the melting ice and

SHORT BERRY CAKE

when we came in, we dutifully hung everything over the steam radiators to dry. What a smell it was with all that wool heating up!

Each house had an icebox in the kitchen where we kept milk, butter, and a few other things that might spoil. Underneath the box was a pan to catch the melting ice, and oh, wow, if someone forgot to empty the pan!

Refrigeration wasn't needed for many things, because below the kitchen we had a vegetable cellar with a cool dirt floor. In it was a potato bin filled with enough potatoes to last all winter. It was a fall ritual to take the Chevy truck to Mr. Peterson's potato farm in White Creek to get them.

Other things were kept in the vegetable cellar, too. Carrots were buried in wooden boxes of sand, and eggs in earthen jars of waterglass (I'm not quite sure what that is!). Shelves were loaded with pickles and preserves and there were a few five-gallon earthenware jars of sweet cucumber pickles, which were my father's favorite. There were no seals on the jars. To get a few pickles, you just stuck your hand in and grabbed a few. It was dark and earthy and wonderful down there and I loved to be sent down to fill the pickle dish before supper.

Another view of the storehouse and foundry (& Uncle Jack)

CHAPTER 4

Nanny

Nanny

My grandmother, Nanny, lived in the house next door to us, which was the family homestead. She was my second mother, but mostly she was my playmate, my mentor, and my friend. Whenever I was scolded or otherwise unhappy, I would run to her for comfort, and she was always there to give it. Like all "farm girls," she loved nature. She taught me to make doll furniture by sticking burdock blossoms together and to make the

SHORT BERRY CAKE

ripe green jewelweed buds pop between my fingers. We raked leaves in the fall with her; picked dandelions for her wine, played hide and seek, and listened to her endless reading. She was pretty, gracious, quiet, sensible, and always had time for family and her many friends.

She was born Martha Galusha on March 13, 1860, in Shaftsbury, Vermont, on a farm which her family called "Holy Smoke." It was at the bottom of a very steep hill. The story is that some member of the family, on seeing it for the first time and preparing to take his wagon down that hill, said, "Holy smoke!"

Richmond & Mary Galusha

Her father, Richmond, was a prosperous farmer, and there are many stories about what a "good" man he was. Her mother was Mary Wheelock, who also came from a long line of staunch, hard-working Vermonters who could trace their lines back to William the Conqueror. Nanny had twin sisters and two brothers.

As a young woman, she taught school in a one-room schoolhouse on the East Road in Shaftsbury. She loved to be driven back to the place, especially on a beautiful fall day when the leaves had turned red and gold. That drive became an annual event.

*A "tintype" of the Galusha children;
Nanny, twin sisters, older & younger brothers*

On March 15, 1888, she married my grandfather, Horatio Clayton Simmons. He worked in the family business in the "big city" of North Bennington. They lived in a small house on "upper" Main Street. Around 1890, they moved to the big house that his father George W. had built. They raised five children and were respected citizens of the town.

In 1918, during World War I, when Nanny's three sons were in the army, my grandfather died. Alone, she managed the business and the property until they returned—and had time to knit hundreds of sweaters for the overseas troops. She continued to manage the three rental houses on the property until 1940 when the business was sold and the property was divided among her three sons.

The Simmons Brothers

The sons, Bernice (William), Jack (Herman), and Chub (Frederick), had houses on the property, so Nanny was able to see four of her five grandchildren grow up.

Our cousin, Clayton Gibson, son of her only living daughter, Carolyn, lived in Springfield, Vermont, at Muckross. He was much older than the four of us, and by the time we came along, he had graduated from Ryan Aeronautical School in Arizona. We didn't know him very well but when he flew alone all the way from San Diego to Bennington, Vermont, we were very proud. His plane was the sister ship of Lindberg's plane, "The Spirit of St. Louis." He dipped and buzzed our house on the way to the airport, and we all waved sheets and towels so he could see us. What an exciting day! The only black spot in the day was his refusal to take any of us cousins up in the plane—he said we might jump out! Really!

Monday, August 1, 1933—Lovely day; Clayton flew over in his plane and took B & M, Fred & M, and Priscilla Norton & Ralph Austin up for a ride and took Mr. Gregg (auto inspector) home with him. Jack having tonsillitis, called Dr. Armstrong.

*Clayton Gibson: with his mother, Carolyn
And a photograph of the pilot*

And later:

September 30, 1933—Clayton flew from Springfield, Vermont, to San Diego, California, in 32 hours of flying time!

SHORT BERRY CAKE

All of her life my grandmother kept a diary in which she noted happenings of the day, the weather, births, deaths, and sicknesses. A very private person, she seldom revealed her emotions or opinions in these diaries—with only a few exceptions.

Monday, April 29, 1935—Marcia turned on refrigerator. No heat today. This meant that the furnace was turned off for the summer.

Monday April 13, 1936—Jack whipped bedroom carpet. This involved dragging the rug outdoors, where it was hung over the clothesline and whipped with a contraption that looked like a large spatula. Billows of dust and dirt that had accumulated over the past year erupted. There were no vacuum cleaners until someone invented the upright "Hoover," but this annual "beating" ritual was a long time dying.

June 25, 1936—We listened on radio to Democratic convention in Philadelphia (rotten) free fight and several injured.

Monday, May 16, 1943—Cool-60—Rain P.M. Carrie left us two years ago today. Oh, how I miss her.

Wed. Dec. 12, 1945—Fair and cold—a beautiful day. Will Woolson's funeral—the last chapter in our once happy days.

Nanny died at the Simmons homestead on May 13, 1947. Hardly a day goes by that I am not reminded of her.

CHAPTER 5

Muckross

Muckross

    Each summer I went with Nanny for a week to visit Aunt Carolyn and Uncle Will in Springfield, Vermont. Their house, called Muckross, was a wonderful replica of a Scottish highland home. It was a nature lover's dream. A massive stone fireplace dominated the living room. From the huge picture windows, we could look down on the long cascading waterfall that tumbled below us. The room smelled of wood smoke and wet moss—with a little of Aunt Carolyn's floral perfume thrown in. She was a horticulturist, and her love for flowers, especially roses, was reflected in every room.

    Stepping off the large porch, I loved to wander by myself down the series of steps and paths leading to the Black River. There were rustic benches along the way; the path was paved and

Mother in Aunt Carolyn's garden

the handrail was covered with pink rambling roses. The path led to a suspension bridge over the river and a shelter on the other side. The river was very wide and the bridge swayed crazily as I walked over it. The shelter was where we waited for the trolley when we went to town.

Shelter by the bridge at Muckross

My favorite place, though, was in a wooded area where the moss was deep and spongy when you stepped on it, and wild

SHORT BERRY CAKE

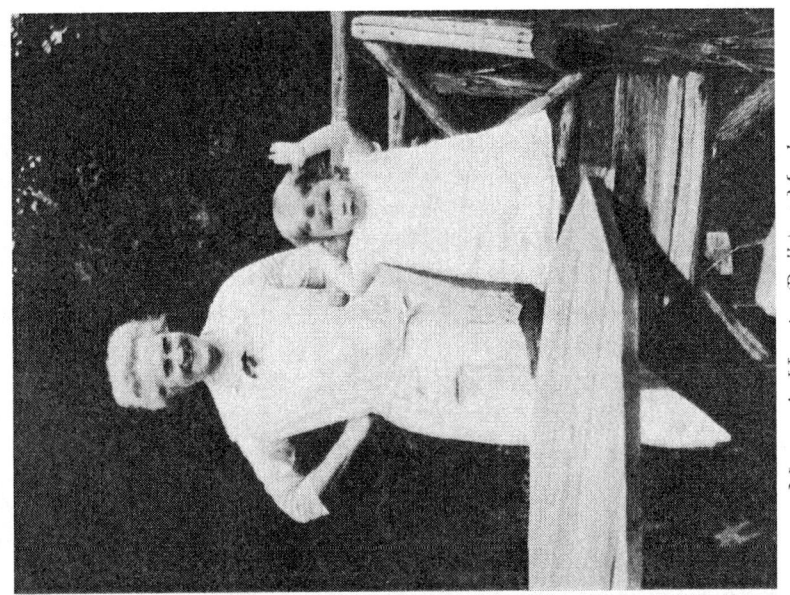

Nanny & Harriet (Polly) at Muckross

Suzanne, my new doll

strawberries grew fat and sweet. Sometimes Nanny and I walked down there, ate berries, then just sat in the swing listening to the birds and squirrels around us. Nanny would whistle to the birds and chickadees would fly down to eat from her fingers.

During these summer visits, I was thoroughly pampered and indulged and I loved it. At the end of our stay, Paul, the chauffeur, took us home loaded down with new toys and elegant clothes and I felt like a queen. Coming back to town and my family was difficult for me, but I'm sure it was more difficult for my mother and everyone else.

Getting back to the three boys soon brought me back to reality, and summer continued.

The Cabin at Muckross

There were many other weekends at Muckross, though they were spent in a less romantic fashion. The property had six hundred wooded acres and three lakes. On a slight bluff above one of the lakes was a wonderful hunting cabin. The roof was covered with sod and had tulips planted in it. In the spring, it looked as if it were straight out of a fairy tale. The cabin was rustic with a stone fireplace in its one big room and tacked on the back was a small kitchen. The furnishings were very primitive,

SHORT BERRY CAKE

but it had bunks for sleeping around three walls. This was where I came with the rest of the family for wonderful weekends, although it was a different world from my visits with Nanny. It always amazed me that the two places never overlapped, and we seldom saw Aunt Carolyn and Uncle Will on these family visits.

We camped out at the cabin many weekends in the summer, fishing in the well-stocked lake, cooking our fish on a kerosene stove, and tramping through the woods picking wintergreen berries. I worried a bit about bears but never saw one. We slept head-to-toe on the bunk beds except for my brother, who was too small. He slept in a bureau drawer!

When Muckross was sold in 1933, it was a sad blow to the whole family. Aunt Carolyn and Uncle Will moved to a beautiful house in town. We continued our family visits, but they involved "dressing up" and "minding our manners" and weren't as much fun.

We did pretty well one Thanksgiving when there were thirteen of us for the weekend. On the big day, the French doors to the dining room were kept closed until dinner was announced—to surprise us all or to keep us out of the kitchen (I never knew which). We had place cards and little china turkey napkin rings at each place, and, of course, several forks and knives and many plates. Coached by glares from our parents, we did pretty well until Delia, the maid, asked Allen if he would have pumpkin or apple pie. He didn't hesitate a minute, but said, "If I was home, I'd have both!" There was dead silence for what seemed like ages, and then everyone talked at once.

About this time, Aunt Carolyn decided it was too embarrassing for her to have us all arrive in the company truck. It was okay at Muckross. Who would notice on six hundred acres? But the house on 11 Summer Hill, in town, was different. So, she bought us a 1936 Dodge sedan to ensure that at least six of us could arrive in style. As far as I can remember, there wasn't another large gathering in Springfield, but every Christmas we came from wherever we were for dinner at our house at 42 Main Street in North Bennington.

SHORT BERRY CAKE

> Dear Santa –
>
> My home is at Mom
>
> It. here in North Bennington and I wanted to let you know what I would like for Xmas. he said you please bring me a new carriage for my Suzanne and some new clothes for her and a nice red raincoat.
>
> My little brother wants a new drum and a train
>
> With love
> Harriett and
> Frederick
>
> I wrote this

Letter to Santa from Harriet

CHAPTER 6

Winter and the Holidays

(Puddin' Hill)

In the winter, when we were very small, our fathers rolled huge snowballs together to make a hill for us to slide down. It worked until the snow got too soft, but we were inventive and soon hollowed out the hill to make an igloo. When we were a little older, we went sliding at Puddin' Hill, as every kid in North Bennington had done for generations. We would come home from school, grab our sled, and go. It was only a city block away. Today the hill looks so very small, but it seemed enormous then. Sliding down was such a thrill and trudging back up the hill again never seemed a chore.

As we got older there was ice-skating, too. The earliest surface to freeze was the "brickyard," which was about a mile walk. I don't know the derivation of its name, but there was a large enough space for a hockey game and it was a shallow, safe place for kids. We thought nothing of walking up there after school at four, which amazes me because surely it was dark by five o'clock!

By the 1930's the radio was beginning to make a big impact on our lives. In the winter, we used to sit on the floor around Nanny's big new Philco radio at five o'clock to listen to Jack Armstrong, the All-American boy, followed by the Lone Ranger. As we ate our breakfast in the morning, we listened to our all-time favorite, Cheerio. I saved Cream of Wheat boxtops for months so that I could join his HCB club and had a diploma to prove it (in case you don't know, it was Hot Cereal Breakfast). How he shaped my character! Even today my idea of heaven is hot oatmeal for breakfast.

Above: Christmas tree picnic. Below: Skiing with the Girl Scouts

Weeks before Christmas, we listened to Santa Claus on Nanny's radio. He read the names of boys and girls he'd been watching with his spyglass all year. He convinced us that we had been good all year and would find presents under the Christmas tree. I don't remember if he read our names, but I always wrote him a letter, AND I got answers each year secretly written by my Aunt Ellen, Mother's sister.

About the first week in December, we took our "big" truck and as many cars as necessary to get Christmas trees. We always went to the Kelly Stand in Arlington where a relative owned land. It was usually snowy, but we built a fire for warmth and to dry our wet wool mittens. It seemed a long process of elimination and we wandered in the woods for hours until we found just the right tree for each family. Finally, when the trees were piled on the truck, we cooked hamburgers, coffee and marshmallows on our bonfire, and rode our sleds down the icy road to the bottom of the mountain without a worry about cars, because the road was closed in the winter.

Family Christmas: 1939

Thanksgiving and Christmas were family holidays and dinner was always at our house. Art, Allen, Frederick, and I always sat at the "children's table." We all eventually graduated to the "big" table, but not until the year that I was married—now I know that it was because the children's table would only seat four.

One Thanksgiving after dinner, when all the adults were asleep in their chairs, we went over to Art and Al's house to make some music. I played the piano and Allen played the violin: "Swinging on the Garden Gate." We never got very far as musicians, and, in fact, I think that was our swan song. I remember I wore a red plaid taffeta dress that Mother had cut off to make a tunic over a navy skirt, and I didn't like it!

Maggie Simmons Sheldon & daughter, Mary Sheldon

SHORT BERRY CAKE

Our favorite place to play on a rainy day was Nanny's attic. Each generation had left its treasures up there. It excited me to think of all the people who had lived here, and with Nanny's help, I knew them all. Actually, she didn't "know" many of them; they had died before she came to the family. But she was the original family historian and she "knew" that Maggie had long black hair, "so long that she could sit on it"; that Mary Sheldon had died at the age of four; and that Great-grandmother Simmons was descended from a laird of Dunbarton Castle. We weren't allowed up in the attic very often, but what a treat it was when we were given permission to go up those winding stairs! The attic, which was appropriately dark and musky, had only one small light at the top of the stairs.

One late winter when we were between seasons (i.e., winter and mud) and getting a little frustrated for something to do, the boys came up with the idea to build a house. We didn't know "how," but that never was a deterrent and the idea really excited us. We began accumulating bits of lumber here and there and started building "the shanty" in Uncle Jack's cellar. This became the "boys' project." I was assigned the job of making curtains for the one window. This was "women's work." The building grew to be about four feet by eight feet and had a peaked roof. As it got higher and higher, my brother remembers thinking, "How do we get it out of here?" But no one mentioned the horrible thought that it might have to be demolished. Once again, we were saved by our fathers. With some ingenuity and some pipes for rollers, they moved it out through the garage doors with half an inch to spare. It was deposited next to the shop where it sat for years. It was a neat place to sit when it was raining. We felt so cozy and protected in there. We played cards, talked a lot, and for lack of anything better to do, the boys pounded nails into an old railroad tie that we had hauled into the place.

Soon other boys were crowding in the shanty. The boys were beginning to talk "dirty." The words "piss" and "shit" had them rolling on the floor with laughter. It made me mad, but I also was getting bored with their silly nonsense.

SHORT BERRY CAKE

Besides, I wanted to do other things. I begged Mother to teach me to crochet. She was making a crocheted pocketbook. It was red and done in a waffle-like pattern. I wanted to make one, too.

"Why don't you start with something simple?" she suggested.

"No," I insisted. "I want to make what you are making."

She consented reluctantly, and I struggled for many weeks until I succeeded and produced a reasonable facsimile of a pocketbook. However, I will never forget that heady feeling of accomplishing the impossible.

After the snow melted, and we got through mud season, one of the most important rites of spring was digging dandelion greens. Usually, the first green tender shoots were dug up at the field in back of Ed Welling's house. They were meticulously cleaned, then boiled with salt pork and new potatoes. It was a meal we all waited for. A few weeks later, Nanny would pass out paper bags for us to fill with the blossoms to use for her dandelion winemaking.

CHAPTER 7

School Days

In September of 1928, I reluctantly went to first grade. The local school, which my father and uncles had attended, was being modernized, so classes were spread out around town until it was finished. My class was held in a room in the bank building. Formerly, it had been the village post office and then Mrs. Haswell's sewing notions store, and I think I resented going to school in a store. It also was very hot in that store and I really wanted to be outdoors. I loved Mrs. O'Neill, who was my teacher, so I soon got over my problem.

Old Post Office and Bank

SHORT BERRY CAKE

As was customary, we had class pictures taken that first week. A man came into the classroom, set up his big camera, put a black cloth over his head, and held up a wooden pallet with an explosive on it. It ignited with an enormous flash, and a portion of the ceiling fell down! We were frightened to death. Understandably, I don't remember another thing about first grade!

By the next fall, classes were held in the "new school," and the first day I was escorted by Carnie White who was one of the "older kids" (she was nine, but I thought she was very grown up and knowledgeable). Carnie and her family had just moved to the house across the street. They formerly lived in the old Lake Paran Hotel on the corner of Bank and Main Streets. She had an older brother, Charles, and a really old sister, Clara—she must have been at least twelve.

Charles White was a part of the birthday party group, but I remember him best walking down the street always whistling, "Bye, Bye, Blackbird." Tall and strong, he was called Blackie. The town was very proud when he got an appointment to West Point. He was in the Pacific at the beginning of the war and was taken prisoner while defending our base on Corregidor. When he later died on the Death March imposed by the Japanese, it was hard to believe; no one in our town was left unaffected by the news.

My teacher in second grade was Miss Meagher, who had a loud voice and used it when a pupil didn't measure up. I was careful to measure up. Our classroom was off the balcony of the gymnasium, so it was fun to come out of the classroom and see the basketball team practicing. There weren't any school buses until we were in high school. Children who couldn't walk to school were brought by their parents and carried lunch boxes. All local students walked home for dinner at noon—it wasn't called "lunch." We were back in school by one o'clock and then had classes until four.

We all loved recess and there were two a day. They only lasted for fifteen minutes, but they were the highlights of our day.

This was where we made friends, argued, gossiped about each other, and exchanged love notes.

My desk in fifth grade was near a window looking out toward a tall elm tree on School Street. When the bell rang for fourth grade recess, I could see the kids running toward that tree, touching it and yelling, "Alley, alley in free." The last one to touch was "it" for the game of hide-and-seek. There were many variations of this old game, but this one was simply for everyone to hide while "it" hid his eyes and counted to one hundred. As the person who was "it" found each person, he had to touch the tree before the person he had found. However, if the hidden one touched first, he was "in free" and "it" had to continue finding people. I have never been able to translate "Alley, alley in free," but we all knew what it meant.

There was always an intense game of marbles, or alleys, as it was later called, going on in a corner of the schoolyard. There were many variations of the game, but it always involved losing or winning some person's prized alley. They were beautiful little balls about a half-inch in diameter. In our fathers' generation they were made of clay and were small terra-cotta balls, but our state-of-the-art alleys were glass with multi-colored swirls inside. Considered very precious, they were carried around in leather bags with drawstring closings. Traditionally, this was a boys' game, so I was not welcome at these contests. Reluctantly, I usually joined the girls who were jumping rope and playing hopscotch on the sidewalk.

Jumping rope could be done singly, but at recess two people turned a long rope and chanted in cadence with the turning rope as a third person jumped. These rhymes were handed down through many generations and everyone knew them.

Teddy Bear, Teddy Bear, turn around
Teddy Bear, Teddy Bear, touch the ground
Teddy Bear, Teddy Bear, show your shoe
Teddy Bear, Teddy Bear, please skiddoo.

Or, how about this one?

> *Call the Army, call the Navy*
> *So-so's gonna have a baby, Wrap it up in tissue paper,*
> *Send it down the elevator (Rope is turned double time)*
> *Boy, girl, twins, triplets, boys, girls, twins, triplets...*

And on and on until the girl jumping missed on the number of babies she was going to have.

When I was eleven, my mother was convinced that I would grow up more gracefully if I had dance lessons. Helen Cushman was the local dance teacher. So, for twenty-five cents a week, I sporadically attended the ballet class. I loved ballet, but sometimes during the Depression, the money was hard to come by. I was not her greatest student, but Miss Cushman introduced me to the world of dance. After trips to Jacobs Pillow to see Ted Shawn, she inspired us to join a class in "interpretive dancing," which was ultimately known as modern dance.

Recital at a garden party in Bennington
I am center front row, Marmie on my right

SHORT BERRY CAKE

My junior year in high school, we were fortunate to have practice teachers from Martha Graham and Hanya Holm's groups. They were in residence at Bennington College, and taught us the basics of modern dance during our physical education classes. Then, for two wonderful summers we could watch and be a part of their practice sessions in our school gymnasium.

I didn't love school—I liked school. Our class had about twenty-five students from first grade through high school. I never was at the top of the class, but managed to hang in near the top half. Looking back, I am amazed at how little we were challenged compared to today's kids. Even in fourth grade, our day consisted of salute to the flag, weekly news events in the class written on the board by a chosen pupil (big deal!), poetry recitations (usually relating to the season), a little arithmetic, taking turns reading to the rest of the class (Dick and Jane?) and penmanship. I am certain there was more that I don't remember and much that prepared me for the era in which I lived.

However, one outstanding teacher and friend in seventh grade civics, Everett Dimmick, did make a big impression. He asked me the definition of "economics" and I was embarrassed to say I didn't know.

"Look it up," he said.

Then, at least every week for the rest of the year I was asked to stand up and say, "Economics is the production, distribution, and consumption of wealth." I have never forgotten!

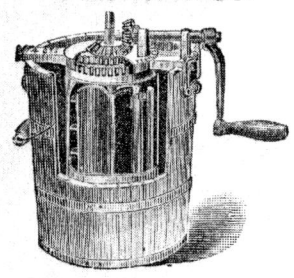

CHAPTER 8

Weekly Schedule

It seemed that the pattern of our days was set by the generation before us and followed the nursery rhyme that we learned in first grade. It went like this:

Sunday, church day
Monday, wash day
Rub-a-rub-a dub
Tuesday, ironing day
Iron, iron, iron
Wednesday, mend day
Sew-a-sew-a-sew
Thursday, bake day
Cook-a-cook-a-cook
Friday, cleaning day
Scrub-a-scrub-a-scrub
Saturday, rest day

On Sunday, nothing interfered with church and Sunday School. Mother sang in the church choir. Daddy was an Easter and Christmas churchgoer, but the rest of the year he stayed home on Sundays and made ice cream ready for us to "crank." It required a lot of preparation. Ice had to be gathered from the spring under the storehouse (which was a big red barn on the property). Ice stayed frozen there until about July. The ice was mixed with rock salt and packed around the custard container in the wooden tub. Homemade custard was then poured into the container and the crank adjusted on the top. After church, we all took turns "cranking"—boring work, but worth it all if you could lick the paddle when it was finished. Oh, what wonderful ice cream it was!

SHORT BERRY CAKE

Monday was washday. The washing machine was in the cellar (not the basement, as it is now called). After being washed, the clothes were put through a wringer that squeezed out the scummy water. The water was hard, detergents hadn't been invented yet, and the released lime really formed a "scum." The clothes were then rinsed in clear water and again wrung out. At this point, shirts, dresses and tablecloths were dipped in a solution of starch, which had been cooked on the stove. Then all were put in the clothesbasket, carried up the cellar stairs and outside—no matter what the weather was like—to be hung on the clothesline. Sometimes in the winter, it took a couple of days to dry; many times Mother had to bend long underwear that was frozen stiff to get it in the clothesbasket.

Tuesday was ironing day and literally everything got ironed. My mother's ironing board was a padded board—one end laid across the kitchen counter and the other end on the children's highchair. First, everything had to be "sprinkled" with water and rolled up to "dampen." Then I loved to watch my mother iron the rough cotton clothes and sheets into silky, smooth recognizable things.

As my mother ironed, she piled up the items that needed mending—that was Wednesday's job. The pile was huge. I doubt that she ever got to the bottom of that pile. Sheets, towels and clothes were made of cotton, silk or wool—there weren't any synthetic fabrics, so the rough washing procedure wore everything out very quickly. Women learned to patch and mend as skillfully as they embroidered.

According to the nursery rhyme, Thursday was bake day. That didn't work for us because Mother, Nanny, Aunt Marcia and Aunt Mammy baked something every day. Weekly, Nanny went to each family to make our supply of doughnuts. The four of us would stand on chairs to watch her cut each strip and poke it into a circle. She always saved enough dough to make "doughney men" for us. They were luscious—hot from the pan and dripping with lard.

SHORT BERRY CAKE

Fridays were cleaning days, and boy, did they clean! Everything was scrubbed and aired, mattresses were "turned" and rugs were "beaten." This was in addition to the annual "spring cleaning," when whole rooms were stripped and the contents washed.

And Saturday—when leftover chores from the week were finished, there was still time for gardening, canning, pickling, berrying, sewing and all the myriad duties that had to be done in an era of hand labor. No one complained about overwork, and it was a great "success" experience to make a perfect apple pie or to remove a stain from a favorite tablecloth.

Life moved at a much slower pace without the pressures of today's world, and there was time while stirring the soup or ironing the sheets to work out one's problems. Psychiatrists, psychologists, awareness programs, philosophy, retreats, and inner vision exercises were unknown to women of these times. They did not have to be taught to "listen, see, and hear of the happenings of spring." The arrival of spring was a part of their lives—the time to dig the dandelions, to hang the curtains in the fresh warm air, and to plant the garden.

Halloween Hoboes—of course our costumes were home-made

CHAPTER 9

The Depression

Life was good.

The Simmons Boiler business was rolling along and we were planning a family swimming pool. It was to be built in back of all three family houses and was to be fed from the spring under the "storehouse" until...

Black Thursday and the financial crash of 1929.

Though the Depression hit parts of the country with a crash, North Bennington, Vermont, limped along for a while; for the most part, our lives went on as usual. We pulled the pool plans and tightened our belts a little. My cat was allowed only ten cents worth of liver once in a while instead of every day. But gradually the family business suffered; extra help was fired and the Simmons Sons were only doing repair work on their previously installed boilers. Mother took a part-time job as a secretary for White's Coal Company, and on the side she wrote news columns for the *Bennington Banner*. Aunt Marcia went to work at Cushman's doing some kind of sewing.

Eventually Mother rented out our bedrooms and ran a boarding house serving dinner at noon. We either bunked out in the "Shelter" (our backyard cabin) or next door at Nanny's. The boarding house idea seemed to be a natural enterprise for my mother. She loved people and was at her best at a party; best of all, she loved to cook. It was a nuisance for us, but in addition to the added revenue, our lives were enriched by contact with many interesting people—schoolteachers, the principal of our high school, the superintendent of schools in our district, members of college glee clubs, but the best for me were members of Martha

SHORT BERRY CAKE

Graham's Dance Group each summer. These people became friends of the family and came back to visit often.

Sunday, March 5, 1933—President Roosevelt closed banks for two days all over the USA.

At this point in the Depression, one in four Americans was out of work. There was no unemployment insurance or food stamps, no government programs to help the poor; most wives didn't work, and when the husband lost his job, all income ceased. Needing cash, people went to their bank accounts to find that the banks were overextended and couldn't meet the demands of the crowds at their doors. This created a "run" on the banks. Many banks failed and some closed temporarily. Roosevelt's bank closing was to create some "breathing space."

Saturday, March 11, 1933—California earthquake. 1000 hurt and hundreds killed. Banks not open yet.

Thursday, March 16, 1933—Milder. Banks opened today for business on restrictions.

Wednesday, March 22, 1933—Carrie gave Harriet $10.00 for birthday. (This was a very generous gift during the Depression!)

August 2, 1933—Jack and Marcia and I sold our old gold pieces to man and woman who were buying old gold. Jack sold H.C.S's gold watch and case $16.30; Marcia's pieces $4.50; Mine: chain, ring $6.82.

During these hard times, one incident stands out in my mind. Mother had gone to Chadwick's store in Old Bennington to buy a box of frozen peas. A company called Bird's Eye had come up with the idea and they were very expensive. When she opened the box, I, of course, was impressed with the idea of peas in winter. My brother, however, remembers how pleased he was that Mother saved the waxed box and cut a liner for his shoes, which had holes in the soles.

SHORT BERRY CAKE

We learned firsthand about poverty and unemployment from the hoboes that frequently stopped at our back door at suppertime to ask for a bite to eat. These hoboes (tramps, as some people called them) were young disillusioned wanderers who "rode the rails" from one town to another. Sometimes they hopped on empty boxcars as they pulled out of the station, but mostly they scrambled to the tops of the cars always keeping one jump ahead of the carknockers who would put them in jail. Their homes were the "jungles" outside of each town, crude campsites where they could make coffee in a tin can over a campfire and find companionship in their misery; the North Bennington jungle was near the coal sheds by the Big Pond trestle. Food was a can of beans heated over the fire or a meal politely begged from houses along the way, marked by some means that we didn't know. My mother and father were very kind to these young men feeling that "there but by the grace of God, go I." And we were intrigued that they were so hungry and so grateful—a world that we didn't know.

November 29, 1933—A letter from Carrie saying they can't draw money out of banks over there. (Carrie was my Aunt Carolyn who lived in Springfield, Vermont. Vermont was now really feeling the effects of the depression.)

My brother, Fred, has added his memories of the time of the Depression:

"I grew up during the Great Depression and World War II. Times were tough because money was hard to come by during the Depression and when it was over, the necessities of life (food, clothing, building material, gasoline, oil, etc.) became scarce since everything was being used to further the war effort.

"The three Simmons families lived in adjoining houses on Main Street in North Bennington, VT. The first house (#40) was the homestead and was occupied by Uncle Jack (Herman M) and Aunt Marcia together with their sons Arthur and Allen (Art and Al). My grandmother Martha G. Simmons (Nanny) lived in a separate part of the house. Next door to this house was #42 occupied by Frederick M.

and Marjorie S. (Fa and Gamma) together with their children Harriet B. (Polly-Sistie to me) and myself. An ell was attached to our house that was a rental apartment (#44). Number 46 was occupied by Uncle Bernie (W. Bernis) and Aunt Mamie (Madiline).

"My grandfather, H.C. (Horatio Clayton, that is) Simmons designed and developed a heating boiler in the late nineteenth century and many of them were installed throughout the northeastern U.S. Upon his death in 1918, the three sons returned from service in World War I and took over the business under the name of H.C. Simmons' Sons. The original boilers were coal fired, but in the late 1920's fuel oil became available and they designed and patented an oil-fired boiler. Unfortunately, this was just before the stock market crash of 1929, and the business suffered until the late 1930s.

"The boilers were built in the shop (now a garage) next door to Uncle Jack's house. When I think back, I am amazed that the three of them could build the boilers without the benefit of power hand tools. They had the heavy machinery to form the various parts, but the assembly was all done with just plain muscle. For example, after the flat steel plate was formed into a cylinder, the two ends had to be joined to make a watertight joint, and this was done by riveting a plate over the resultant seam. Red-hot rivets heated in a small forge were inserted through previously drilled holes in the plate and the cylindrical shell. The rivet protruded slightly through the plate and with one of the men bearing down on a quite long handled sledgehammer propped up at the head to "buck" the rivet, the other two men took alternate blows with sledgehammers to head it over. There must have been close to a hundred rivets and I think I probably saw one of the last built in this manner because later they had a welder from Troy, New York, do the job.

"The rolling stock consisted of a circa late twenties Model T Ford roadster and a Graham truck of about the same vintage. The Model T was made into a pickup truck by removing the bustle back trunk and replacing it with a box. The Graham truck, which we kids referred to as the "Big Truck," had a box about eight or ten feet long and about three feet deep. I gather that the Model T was used for personal use by whoever needed it as it was before my arrival on the scene. I believe that Gamma was transported to the hospital in it when I was about to arrive. I can't imagine what it must have been like in the dead of winter with only the heat coming off the exhaust manifold for warmth. The Model T was retired in 1931 and replaced with a Chevrolet coupe that was modified in the same manner as the Model T.

"I believe the effects of the Depression were not felt by the Simmons families until 1933 or 1934. Actually, we had it pretty good compared to some of the other people in the village. We had central heating fired with an oil burner, hot and cold running water, indoor plumbing, and an electric range and electric refrigeration, while other people were burning coal for heat and hot water, using ice boxes for refrigeration, and outhouses for answering the call to nature. Aunt Millie and Uncle Walter Cole, who lived on the outskirts of the village towards Shaftsbury, had a huge cast iron kitchen range for cooking and making hot water plus a parlor stove, both of which were coal-fired and the only sources of heat for the house. In the winter they lived in the kitchen and parlor (living room), the rest of the house unheated except for a small amount of heat that reached the bedrooms upstairs through registers in the ceiling. There was a single cold water tap in a cast iron kitchen sink; if you wanted hot water, you dipped it out of the reservoir at the end of the stove. Saturday night baths were taken in a washtub in the kitchen. To answer the call to nature, you either went to the outhouse attached to the barn, or, if it was the middle of the night, used the chamber pot in the bedroom. Some people had kerosene stoves for cooking that operated on much the same principle as a kerosene lamp, but of course the burners were much larger. You could tell who used them because the whole house smelled of kerosene.

"I guess the thing that really brought home to me how bad things were was an incident that happened when I was probably eight or nine years old. I used to hang out at a garage across the tracks from the railroad station. The son of the owner was always fooling around with cars, model airplanes, a powered iceboat, and just about anything mechanical. Anyway, one evening I was up there and a young man appeared carrying a crescent wrench and asked if they would buy it so he could buy some milk for his baby. That really shook me up. He was refused; I can still see him walking back down the street with his wrench. Thinking about the baby, I had trouble sleeping that night.

"Those who were employed worked either at H.T. Cushman Company, which made colonial furniture; the H.C. White Company, manufacturers of children's wooden vehicles of various sorts; and the A.S. Payne Company, who made wooden hand mirrors. Sometime in the late thirties, a law was passed setting the minimum wage at forty cents an hour, which meant a paycheck of sixteen dollars for a forty-hour week. Not a lot to live on . . . remember, most of the women (mothers) weren't gainfully employed but took care of the home front where, I might add, they worked their fingers to the bone managing the household. Both the H.C. White Company and the A.S. Payne Company went 'belly up' before the end of the Depression.

"Since he was the eldest of the three men, Uncle Bernie used to come around every Saturday with the week's pay. I recall on one occasion when I was old enough to have some idea of the value of money, he handed Gamma a ten-dollar bill for the week. Not very much, but when you consider the following, it was possible to get by. For example, bananas were four pounds for a quarter or about six cents a pound, and, in a 1936 Sears catalog, wool suits were selling for about sixteen dollars. In a recent flyer from one of the supermarkets, bananas were advertised at fifty-nine cents a pound, and I guess you can probably buy a suit for a hundred and fifty to two hundred dollars. In other words, a dollar then was worth ten dollars in today's money. I say it was possible to get by, but we had no mortgage or rent to pay since all of the houses were part of H.C. Simmons' estate.

"To augment the family income, Gamma took in boarders, usually schoolteachers, and, since there were only three bedrooms in the house, I was shuffled around to make room for them, finally ending up in the cellar in what was once a playroom Fa had made for us. I liked it because it was like having my own private hideaway where nobody would bother me. Gamma was also the North Bennington correspondent for the Bennington Evening Banner and wrote a column about the goings on in the village at five cents per inch of column.

"There were four grocery stores on Main Street, three of them not more than a couple hundred feet from the house. Dwyer's Market was in the brick building now occupied by the Villager Restaurant. The A&P was about fifty feet down the street, and Powers and Robinson was

SHORT BERRY CAKE

across the street next to the bank building. Sheperd's (Buck Buchanan's grandfather) store was at the foot of Main Street. There were no supermarkets until after the war. You gave the clerk your order and he collected the food, brought it back to the counter, and totaled up the cost on the paper bag he put the groceries in. Sometimes Gamma would call in the order and send me down to pick it up. Once a week, Powers and Robinson would deliver large orders to outlying areas, and we always knew when it was so we could ride around with them making the deliveries. Our food was purchased on an "as needed" basis. I would like to have a nickel for every time that I had to respond to "Pete, go down to the store and get a loaf of bread." I was "Pete" to Gamma until I graduated from college as a "promising young engineer." I was still her promising young engineer when she was ninety years old.

"All of the canned goods and dry goods were displayed on shelves that were perhaps ten feet tall; the can or box was retrieved with a long handled clamping device. Meat was displayed in a glass front case, and after you made a selection, the clerk picked it up with his bare hand, wrapped it in butcher's paper, wiped his hands on his apron, and took it to the counter. If you didn't see what you wanted, he went to the walk-in cooler at the back of the store, brought out a chunk of meat and carved off what you wanted. Cookies were displayed in a transparent topped canister, and again the clerk reached in with his bare hand to retrieve your selection. If you wanted freshly ground hamburger, they would grind the required amount. After they finished, they would wipe off the end of the grinder with their fingers and plop it on top of the pile. No latex gloves, but we survived!

"The only foods that were purchased were dairy products, meat, and staples such as sugar, flour, bread, etc. There were no mixes that required only the addition of milk or foods of the "heat and serve" variety. Back then; if you asked somebody if something were made from "scratch," you'd get nothing but a blank look as if to say, "What are you talking about?" Fa had a vegetable garden and Gamma used to spend a lot of the time in the late summer canning all kinds of vegetables that were put down in the vegetable cellar. Anything that wasn't produced in the garden was purchased from a local farmer. Every fall Fa an I would journey to Jimmy Peter's farm over near White Creek, NY, and purchase six or eight bushels of potatoes, a bushel of Northern Spy apples, a couple of Blue Hubbard squash (a small one was the size of a basketball), and whatever else caught Fa's eye. In addition, we went to a local cider mill to fill an old five-gallon Coca Cola syrup keg that was put in the vegetable cellar where the cider fermented through the winter so Gamma would have plenty of vinegar for the following year's pickles.

"In the summer there were several peddlers who came around selling various kinds of fresh produce. Phoebe Bump from Shaftsbury Hollow sold wild blueberries and horseradish. And then there was Dewey Bronson who ran a market in South Shaftsbury and came around in his pickup truck with a homemade cab on the back containing various cuts of meat. He never knocked on the front door but just walked through the house to the kitchen where Gamma could always be found. He'd announce, "Marge, I have some nice pork today." Then they would walk out to the truck where he would cut whatever she wanted. Dewey always had a cigar tucked in the corner of his mouth and you could always tell when he had been there because the house smelled of cigar smoke. He only showed up during cool weather because there was no refrigeration in his truck.

"Milk was delivered to our back door in glass quart bottles. During the winter, if it wasn't retrieved fairly soon, the milk froze and pushed the waxed cardboard cap out of the top so it looked like a little top hat. This was pasteurized milk (homogenization had not yet arrived), so the cream would separate out and collect in the top of the bottle. Gamma had a gadget that was dropped in the top of the bottle and would siphon the cream off to be used in their coffee. Later, a new type of bottle made its appearance, appropriately called a "cream top bottle." It looked like an oversized hourglass except that the bottom portion was much larger than the top, which was sized to collect the separated cream—perhaps one-half to three-quarters of a cup. A small round spoon supplied by the dairy was lowered into the bottle to close off the neck between the top and bottom sections; holding the spoon tight against the neck, you simply poured off the cream. I would still like to know how the first gadget worked.

"We ate well. Gamma could always come up with something delicious made from the most basic ingredients. To some people, the

SHORT BERRY CAKE

thought of eating fried salt pork with milk gravy on a baked potato, together with boiled dandelion greens would surely make them gag. Generally our meals consisted of the meat, potato, and vegetable variety, but Gamma always did something that all good cooks do: gave the food a little extra something that makes it out of the ordinary. Some time in the late thirties or early forties we were served spaghetti and meatballs (the stuff the Italians eat). Gamma made the best meat sauce imaginable; later on in my travels I found few Italian restaurants that made sauce equal to it. One of our economy meals included spare ribs; I have to chuckle when I see the price of them today. Sunday dinners were always rather sumptuous and always included a roast or some kind of a steak that Fa would broil on the outdoor fireplace.

"Because of the tough financial times, we saved everything from newspaper to string. At the foot of the cellar stairs was a big box where all the newspapers were deposited; periodically an 'old-timer' would come around in his Model A Ford truck to pick them up. I don't know if he paid for them, but if he did, it probably wasn't more than twenty-five cents. Also, there was a box near the laundry, and every piece of textile material that had outlived its usefulness was held there. If I remember correctly, the cotton material was saved until there was a sufficient quantity of various colors to make braided rugs and the woolen material was saved until there was enough to send to the Olsen Rug Company. For X pounds of woolen rags you could buy a carpet of a given size very inexpensively. I think a nine-by-twelve carpet was purchased for one of the rooms this way.

"As I write, I realize just how little "stuff" was thrown away. At one time there was a garbage pit behind the barn in back of Uncle Jack's house where the three families dumped their garbage. Later this was replaced with three twenty-five or thirty gallon drums enclosed in a small shed. It used to get pretty ripe around there, especially in the summer, but the point I'm making is that those drums were taken to the dump no more than once every couple of months. Way out in back of Uncle Bernie's house were two steel cylinders about four feet in diameter and three or four feet deep. One of them was used as an incinerator for burning papers and the other was for tin cans and glass containers. There was no plastic of any kind to dispose of. The only glass containers to be dumped were those like ketchup or mayonnaise bottles. The glass milk bottles were washed and left on the back steps for pickup at the next delivery. Soda was sold in glass bottles and the price included a deposit of two cents for a small bottle and five cents for a quart bottle. Finding a quart bottle of that type was like finding money because if you took it to the store the deposit would buy a double dip ice cream cone. Only once a year would the men empty all of the rubbish generated by the three families into the "Big Truck" and haul it to the dump. When I see the amount of rubbish generated by this generation, it makes me wonder.

"There was only one homeless person in the village that I can think of. "Big Bill McCarthy" had been a motorman on the trolley cars that ran through the village prior to 1927. I don't know what he did after the demise of the trolleys, but at the time I knew of him, he was a hopeless alcoholic and lived (slept) in the basement of the railroad station. During the day he hung out at Panos' store (more about the store later). And then there were the hobos or tramps also referred to as "Knights of the Open Road" who carried everything they owned in a bedroll of sorts. These were men who were unemployed and rode the rails in the freight cars in search of work. Because our house was so close to the railroad, it was not uncommon for one of them to appear at the front door asking for a "handout." Sometimes they would offer to do some work around the yard in return. All of these men were not bums. Some of them we talked to were quite intelligent but just down on their luck. Gamma would make them a sandwich and a cup of coffee and they would sit on the back steps to eat it. Needless to say, they all disappeared with the coming of winter and headed for a warmer climate. North Bennington had a reputation among these as a good place for a soft touch."

CHAPTER 10

Summer

& Short Berry Cake

Wednesday, May 30, 1934—Lovely warm day. Boys put up flag. Very nice parade. I took off underwear. (My grandmother was a very proper lady; she only meant that the weather was now warm enough to change from winter long underwear to the light summer variety)

Memorial Day marked the beginning of the summer and we were all up early to watch our fathers "put up" the big American flag. It was made of wool. I remember Nanny sitting in a chair on the lawn with the flag draped over her lap, mending places where the moths had done their damage. My grandfather had acquired the flag in payment for a debt owed him by a man in North Adams. It spanned the street from the peak of Nanny's house to a tall elm tree on the Tobin property across the street. It had thirty-eight stars and it was always a challenge to guess what year that flag was made. Getting the thing up was a family project, and a risky one.

My cousin, Allen, recalls one particular Memorial Day and his experience with the flag. In his words:

"*I was home on furlough from the US Army during the second World War. I awoke on Memorial Day, dressed in my uniform, and stepped outside to the raising of the enormous flag to be hung directly above the street. By then, half the town was watching the event. Of course, I was happy to be watching too.*

"*We lived in a two-and-a-half story house on the center of Main Street in this small town (population one thousand). At the peak of the gable on the house was a pulley with a rope hanging with the ends tied to the silcock near the ground. This rope was left there all year. On the*

SHORT BERRY CAKE

opposite side of the street was a large tree with a heavy branch horizontal with a pulley on it. The rope on that side could not be left all year round hanging in mid-air, so it had to be put up at each hanging.

"I was still enjoying watching my father and his two brothers unfold the flag and tie the rope to each end of the flag. Then they put up their thirty-foot extension ladder under the pulley in the tree. They set it straight up, but the ladder was about two feet short of reaching the pulley.

"Suddenly, everybody looked at me and said, 'You're going up the ladder!'

"What! All in their fifties, my dad was about five-feet ten and his two brothers were shorter. The three of them held the ladder and waited for me. I didn't like heights—especially under these conditions. But since I was young and in uniform and half the town was watching, I had to suck it in and climb the ladder. My job was to carry the rope up to put through the pulley. The higher I got, the heavier the thick rope became. About three-quarters the way up, the ladder started to sway . . . back and forth . . . back and forth.

"When I looked down, my gang holding the ladder looked like ants. I have never been as scared as much as I was at that moment. I kept climbing and praying as I reached the top.

"Now what was I supposed to do? The pulley was still two feet above me. The ladder was really swaying and the rope was unbelievably heavy.

"I finally reached up and put the end of the rope through the pulley, then thought, Now what? I couldn't use my other hand to pull it through because I was hanging onto the ladder for dear life with that arm. With another prayer, I managed to inch the rope through the pulley with my fingers. It seemed to take forever to get it through long enough to reach my other hand.

"The crowd gave a big yell at my success, and I was able to get down quickly. We pulled the ropes on each pulley and our fig flag was centered over the street.

"It was always a great thrill to see all the marching parades and everyone saluting the flag. After that, I arranged my furloughs at a different time. But in later years, the local firemen did the job of displaying the flag and we all breathed a sigh of relief."

Our Flag: always displayed at Memorial Day celebrations

    The flag has only thirty-eight stars and dates back to 1876 when Colorado became the thirty-eighth state to enter the union. It was given to my grandfather, H.C. Simmons, around the turn of the century and was flown over Main Street for over sixty-five years, except for two years during World War I. It is now reposing in the Bennington, Vermont Museum.

    Family and friends began to gather on our front porch to get a "good view" as we waited for hours, it seemed, for the parade to begin. Each year it was an exciting event with the high school band led by Mrs. Porter, the school music teacher; then the Boy Scouts, the Girl Scouts, the war veterans (from the Civil War,

Spanish American War, and WW1) and long lines of school children waving little American flags marched by. Weaving in and out of the parade were boys on bikes decorated with red, white and blue crepe paper wound around the spokes of the wheels. The parade went up Main Street to the cemetery where some dignitary gave a speech, an honored person gave the Gettysburg Address, and someone read, "In Flanders Field the poppies grow between the crosses row on row . . .." The part that still gives me shivers was the playing of "Taps" and way off in the distance, its echo. It was a tough act for our inexperienced high school buglers and sometimes the echo wasn't exactly an echo, but we were all forgiving. When it came to patriotic fervor and enthusiasm, the fourth of July got top billing.

For our parents, the holiday started on the "Night before the Fourth" with a barbecue in the backyard. We were put to bed early to rest up for the next day—they said! At midnight, there was usually an impromptu parade up Main Street, led by Ed Nash, with his slide trombone, and we crept to the window to watch. Next morning we were up early and out on the back porch with our packets of firecrackers. There were about twenty crackers in a package with the fuses neatly entwined. We carefully undid them as our fathers had shown us so we could light one cracker at a time and make them last longer.

We each had a stick of "punk" for lighting the fuses. When it was lit, it burned slowly like incense. We took each cracker, lighted it with the punk, threw it off the back porch, held our ears, and waited for the big boom. The ultimate excitement was to put a tin can over a cherry bomb, light the fuse, run, and watch as the can was shot into the air. In our arsenal, we also had cherry bombs, snakes and sparklers. The town sounded like a battlefield, with explosions going off all day, leaving clouds of smoke and a smell of sulfur in the air. The day was usually hot and we took a breather, now and then, to run through the lawn sprinkler in our bathing suits. By afternoon we were out of ammunition and could hardly stand the wait for the exciting event in the evening.

Wednesday, July 4, 1934—Lovely day. Community fireworks put on by Jack and Fred and Bud (Ralph) Norton. GOOD! Well attended. Mrs. W. White and Miria Endress my guests. Over 200 people in yard.

Each year my father, Uncle Jack, and their friend Bud Norton collected a dollar from each family in town to buy Roman candles, skyrockets, and other fancy "pieces." They worked for weeks building ramps and platforms and troughs to shoot the things from; on the big night, they took turns lighting the fuses. Fortunately, no one was hurt but it surely was a miracle. The wait until it was dark enough for the fireworks was interminable. So, just at dusk, skyrockets were shot into the air and from them came little toy men with parachutes. We caught them as they

Mother and Daddy on Memorial Day

came down and each child had one to keep. Then the big show began and it really was remarkable. The "rockets' red glare and the bombs bursting in air" were as awesome to us as the ones seen by Francis Scott Key. As each rocket burst in the sky, there were "ooh's" and "ah's" from the appreciative crowd and the show was never long enough. The finale was traditionally a huge

SHORT BERRY CAKE

American Flag, composed of red, white and blue sparklers on a framework built by our fathers. When it was lit, we all cheered.

Sunday, July 23, 1934—Hot 90°. Jack and Fred's families went blueberrying over on East Road. Got about 20 qts.

In the summer, berry-picking was constant. I used to know the meadows where the best strawberries grew, and I noticed that they always grew near a patch of daisies. The biggest raspberries grew in Shaftsbury Hollow, and the best blackberries on the East Road near the location of Nanny's one-room schoolhouse. Blueberries were plentiful on the West Mountain and in the fall, there were butternuts on the Sunderland Hill Road. It was always a challenge to see who could pick the most, but what did we do with that many blueberries?

Girl Scouts and Wildflowers—Back row (l to r): Virginia Babson, Me Front: Pauline Sanborn, Helen Hill, Barbara Powers, Arlene Sanborn

Our mothers canned and preserved constantly all summer in preparation for the long cold winters. It was a necessity since fresh fruits and vegetables were non-existent from November until June. The most delicious smells always came from my mother's kitchen in the summer, and they varied with the season. In June the sweet smell of berry jams bubbling on the stove; in July, the smell of hot vinegar being poured on tiny gherkins for pickles; and August brought sweet peaches being boiled in sugar syrup. Probably the most nostalgic smell of all, though, was the one that pervaded the house from August until the first frost in September. Who can ever forget chili sauce? Even now, on a chilly fall day, I love to cook up a little, just for that heady aroma.

The same greedy rationale held for picking wildflowers, but the need was purely esthetic or maybe "to feed our souls." But from the first hepatica in the spring to the last bittersweet in the fall, we brought home as many as we could carry. We utilized every available container; the house would be full of wildflowers in jelly jars, pitchers, and even an occasional tin can. In the fall Nanny always had two large Bennington Pottery jars filled with Queen Anne's Lace and Goldenrod on the steps by her front door.

One cold early spring day in April 1934, I went after school to McCullough's woods alone to see if any spring flowers were in bloom. The wind was blowing hard, making strange noises as it blew against an old wire fence. When I heard the eerie noise, I remembered news reports I'd heard that the worst desperado in US history, John Dillinger, was still at large. I was certain that if I were he, I would hide in McCullough's woods. Just as I discovered a large patch of the deepest blue hepaticas, the fence squeaked and waved in the wind. I panicked. Should I pick or run? I ran. I later heard that John Dillinger was killed outside a bar in July in Chicago—a long way from McCullough's Woods in North Bennington.

There was no television, but we did have limited radio in the evening from a crystal set and a big horn that amplified the sound. We listened to the National Barn Dance from Chicago. One night my father went up to the railroad station and sent them a telegram saying, "Way back in Vermont we enjoy your program." We waited with bated breath, and sure enough, they read the telegram on "the air." What a wonderful invention the radio was!

Calvin Coolidge shaking the hand of "Punk" Sinay at the North Bennington station as he returns to Washington following the death of President Harding, August 2, 1923.

SHORT BERRY CAKE

A family named Sinay lived in one of our tenement houses near the railroad tracks; the house was known with much glee by the local folks as the "Simmons Back House."

Behind the house was an old sour cherry tree that was loaded with wonderful sour cherries. The house was torn down about 1929, but the cherry tree still survived. We once thought up a plan to get rich quick. We picked cherries all day (I had to beat on the boys a bit for this one), set up a table on the Main Street sidewalk to sell our produce, and took turns manning the sales. This enterprise didn't last long; we didn't get rich, and we learned early that the compensation was not worth the work.

Our favorite pastime—or at least my favorite—was our shows. These were circuses usually, and I was the trapeze artist, swinging upside down in our old elm tree from a trapeze made of a broomstick and some clothesline. We gave plays, too. In our homemade tent made of two blankets thrown over the clothesline, we produced Charlie's Aunt long before it hit Broadway. Being the oldest, I, of course, was the director. Mother used to tell the story of hearing us practice one hot summer when all the boys had whooping cough. As each boy would have an attack of coughing and go outside the tent to throw up, the rest of us never stopped our rehearsal. Even then, the show had to go on!

There always was so much to do, and the days never seemed long enough. We would go out to play in the morning and play all day—as long as we showed up for meals and came home in the evening when the streetlights came on.

Imagine, no one was able to reach us all day—there were no cell phones, or even any telephones. We were out there in the cold, cruel world without a guardian or a parent to tell us what to do. We ate cupcakes, bread with lots of butter, drank sugar soda (with four friends on one bottle), but we didn't die from it, and we were never overweight. No video games, no computers, no radio, but we had each other and friends. We made up games with sticks and tennis balls; we fished in the big pond, explored in the barn, and once, when a Pullman car was left on the siding, we went up to the station and pretended to be trainmen.

Things didn't seem to be planned. They just happened. Climbing trees was a great activity and we spent many hours building platforms in them. I still remember getting to the top of a tall pine tree to look out on the world below—no astronaut would ever have a greater thrill. We of course, argued and teased each other—especially the boys against me—but we managed to get over the arguments without the help of parents or psychiatrists.

Each year we looked forward to the day when the "Fresh Air Kids" would arrive from New York on the train. Many families in the town applied to have underprivileged children from the city live with them for two weeks in the summer. Almost the whole town turned out to greet them at the station with a mixture of genuine warmth and morbid curiosity to see how they had changed from last year. We came to know them all, and we liked to believe that the transformation from bedraggled, scared, undernourished little kids to confident, happy teenagers was due to their two-week stint in Vermont each year.

One little boy stands out in my memory. He came each year to stay with two elderly widows who were sisters, Mrs. Cora Welling and Mrs. Ann Henry. They lavished love and care on little Jonas and he reciprocated with appreciation and affection, even when they washed his head with kerosene to remove the lice. One Sunday our family took him on a picnic to Lowell Lake, a favorite lake in Londonderry. We rented a boat and took turns rowing around the lake; it was a new experience for him, and after watching us maneuver around the water for a while, he said, "Hey, give me one of those shovels." He came for many summers, returning to the city each year with a new haircut, new clothes, many toys, and a little fatter. He was such a happy, smiling child, and we all were sad when he left. I wonder where he is now.

The Shelter was a one-room cabin that my father had built on the back of the property. It was screened on three sides, had a peaked roof, a wide overhang (so we weren't bothered by rain), and smelled deliciously of creosote. My brother and I slept out there until about the end of October, but Mother and Daddy usually gave up by Labor Day. It was the finest sleeping I have ever encountered. One night in October, I had gone to bed early—in the Shelter. My mother and father were asleep in the house and as my brother Frederick came home late from a school function, a neighbor stopped him and said that a man had been seen entering our house (we never locked the doors). Frederick quietly opened the door in the dark and with the light from the moon could see a pair of shoes on my father's footstool. Our hero did a flying tackle, pulled the man to the floor and pinned him down. All the time the man was yelling, "Hey, what do you think you're doing? Get outta here!"

It took a while to sort things out, but the upshot was that the man had rented the house from my grandfather thirty years earlier and this night had too many beers and thought he would just go home and put his feet up and he did—thirty years too late!

In the summertime, we ate many meals outside at our backyard picnic table and my father did much of the cooking on the stone fireplace that he had built. It was a long trek from the house to the table carrying all the necessary implements, but my mother and father considered it worthwhile and we didn't object. I must admit, though, that about the fourth time I was sent "back to the house" to get the milk or the butter or the salt, I was a little exasperated and sulked noticeably. But now, I think back to how pleasant it was and how far ahead of the time my parents were. I suspect that many people considered us a little "far out," although Mother's informal invitations were sought after—even to breakfast in the backyard when she served elephant ears! (These were bread dough left over from yesterday's bread making, stretched out to the size of your hand and fried in butter. They were spread with lots of strawberry jam and served hot).

Art recalls one of our summer cookouts—family and neighbors had gathered and the party was in full swing. Bud

SHORT BERRY CAKE

Norton, our good friend and neighbor, was working late at the bank and hadn't appeared yet. As darkness approached, my father started cooking the steaks and the picnic table was spread with Mother's salads and home baked breads. At this point, Bud arrived at his apartment on Bank Street, changed his clothes and hurried to the picnic, taking the shortcut through our adjoining hedgerow, going behind our barn and about a hundred yards to where the steaks were cooking. It was very dark, but he could see the glow from the fire. He knew the way and was certain the location of our compost trench was between him and the party. This compost trench was a dug hole about six feet by three feet and two feet deep where all the families dumped garbage through the year. It was periodically watered and turned to keep it decomposing for use on our gardens the next spring.

So Bud hurried on, confident that he was on familiar ground and—of course—tripped and fell face down in the gooey, slurpy mess. For anyone, this would be a horrible experience, but for Bud, who was a fastidious man, it must have been devastating. We don't remember whether he had any steak, but we do remember that the next day we were assigned the job of searching in the slurp for Bud's glasses—which we triumphantly found.

Our evenings were longer in those days because we had supper about five o'clock, and that meant many hours before bedtime (daylight savings time hadn't been invented yet). In the summer after supper, parents and their kids would sometimes gather for a rousing game of Kick the Can, baseball, or croquet. The Simmons "backyard" was a gathering place for kids of each generation and people just "showed up." I remember counting fifteen bicycles one afternoon leaned up against the barn.

One Sunday in early spring after church, we drove to Shaftsbury with Nanny to visit the Galushas. Nanny's brother Marcus and his wife Austia lived in a little red house on the Galusha farm. Across the road, lived his son Horace, wife Lola, and children Olive, Charlotte, and Warren. As we pulled in the yard, Charlotte, who was my age, came running to meet us.

SHORT BERRY CAKE

"Oh, I'm so glad you came," she said." We went berrying today, and Mother made Short Berry Cake!" Henceforth, that harbinger of spring—strawberry shortcake—had a new name in our family. But never again has it been so wonderful—the berries were not from a grocery store but were tiny wild berries that had been handpicked from the meadow. Aunt Lola's shortcake was made from scratch, of course, and light as a feather; the cream was lavish and must have been a hundred percent butterfat.

After dinner, there was much news to catch up on, so while our parents visited, we went across the road with Charlotte and Warren to the barn to jump in the hay. Hay was not put in bales as it is today, but tossed loosely in the barn. It was very exciting to climb up in the rafters and leap down into a pile of soft, sweet-smelling hay—we did it over and over. Slacks for girls were unheard of, so of course I jumped in my Sunday dress and my legs itched all the way home. But it was worth it. Our visits always seemed to end too soon.

Arthur, Allen, Polly, and Bud-Dog

If all else failed in the evening, it was pleasant to sit and rock with Nanny on her front porch that faced Main Street. The evenings were quiet except for cicadas in the trees on a hot night. We could hear Mike (later known as Larry) Powers whistling as

SHORT BERRY CAKE

he walked up the street or Big Bill McCarthy staggering up the street toward the station talking to some unknown figment of his alcoholic imagination. And in the background, we usually heard the sound of Percey Hynick playing his harmonica as he sat on the station loading platform.

At the end of a hot summer day after swimming most of the day at the "Big Pond," I would love to sit on our cool concrete porch steps and wait for the paper boy to deliver our local newspaper, the *Bennington Evening Banner*. I would spread it out on the porch floor, turn the page to the comics and devour the lives of Tillie the Toiler, Barney Google, and Winnie Winkle, the Breadwinner. Tillie and Winnie were the working girls of the 20s; they were virtuous, hardworking, and usually the sole support of a loving mother and a ne'er-do-well father and numerous kids. Tillie had a boyfriend whom she periodically stood up whenever a better-looking guy came along. Winnie, on the other hand, had a boyfriend who adored her, but he was a kind of nerd.

On Sundays, we would gather on Uncle Jack's "side" porch or in our backyard to read the comics in the *Boston Globe*—pages

Reading the Sunday Funnies

and pages of funnies with soap-opera type stories that we followed avidly. There were the Katz 'n Jammer Kids, The Gumps, Toots and Casper, and who can forget Gasoline Alley, where Walt, Bill, Doc, and Avery worked on their cars on weekends? And remember Barney Google and his beloved horse Spark Plug? Barney loved to chase showgirls when he wasn't being henpecked by his wife—"the sweet woman"—and he ran for president!

We, of course, didn't realize that we were reading a story of our times. During World War I, women began working outside the home, and after the men returned home, the economy allowed many to keep working. By 1921, eight million American women held jobs outside the home, automobiles replaced horses, the middle class grew and prospered, the movies began to talk, women won the right to vote, and radio was born.

There was a change of values in America—especially in the female population. Young women rejected their parents' Victorian values. They stopped wearing corsets, bobbed their hair, wore makeup and shorter skirts, and took up smoking and drinking. The style was art deco, the dress was the flapper, and the dance was the Charleston—and the newspaper comics documented it all.

Polly and Bud-Dog

We had a dog; I think he actually belonged to Uncle Jack, but we all considered him "ours." Called Bud-Dog, he was part collie and part shepherd. For breakfast he had coffee and doughnuts, but wouldn't eat while anyone was watching (no one had thought of "dog food" in those days. They ate what we ate). Bud-Dog was our constant companion and took part in all of our activities. When we climbed trees, he sat and watched; when we played board games, he slept at our feet; when we went swimming—nearly every day in the summer—he went too. He loved to dive from the high dive at Lake Paran—which the pond came to be called—and didn't seem to mind swimming around with us holding onto his tail.

"Fregit" and "Hyatt"

We always had one or two cats, but once we had two rabbits. Our fathers built a super cage for them out of a big shipping crate. It wasn't long before we had ten rabbits with evidence that more were on the way. It was my turn to clean the cage on the day that Underwood and Underwood, the fancy New York photographers, were arriving to photograph us. I was bathed and brushed and wore a clean starched dress, but then I remembered the rabbits; it was my turn to clean the cage. So I slipped out to the barn and crawled in the cage, but no rabbits. I was frantic. They had simply disappeared. I have always suspected that the uncles couldn't face more rabbits, but no one looked guilty, so I was convinced the mother had found a better home for them. I was dragged in for the picture taking, but even now I think of my rabbits whenever I see that picture.

One day when I was about ten, there was a lot of excitement in the shop because a professional photographer was coming to take pictures of the H.C. Simmons & Sons. This was a promotional idea to give the company a new image. After snapping several shots of the uncles, my father, and their one worker, Wilbur Caroll, someone said, "Oh, we must now have one of the future crew."

Great idea! So the four of us scrambled up to the trucks when the photographer said, "Not her. She's a girl." Everyone looked at me as though they had never noticed before, and then someone said, "Oh, you're right. Girls don't do this kind of work." I was embarrassed and hurt and really mad as I stormed away to Nanny.

I felt that discrimination was creeping into our family, and then the worst happened. One day when I was "Indian wrestling" with some unsavory boys on my grandmother's front lawn, I was called into the house. From the tone of my mother's voice, I could tell it was going to be bad. And it was! I was told that such behavior would no longer be tolerated. I was to behave like a young lady (whatever that was). I was not to wrestle with the boys, climb trees, or sleep in their tent—what a blow! Mother didn't explain "why" and I never asked. How differently my granddaughters would react today!

Publicity Photo of H.C. Simmons Sons

Anyway, I was devastated, but not for long—I soon discovered Girl Scouts.

Saturday, October 21, 1933—Harriet gone on hike with scouts over to cave on Mt. Anthony

The captain of the troop in North Bennington was Marian White. We called her Miss Marian. About thirty-five, she was a wonderful outdoors person, an avid hiker, an amateur naturalist, and she opened our eyes to the world. She brought people from all walks of life to help us with merit badges. She found nurses, electricians, carpenters, bankers, dancers, and many others who were willing to share their knowledge with us. We learned to identify wildflowers, to do contra dancing, to weave a basket, to sculpt a bar of Ivory soap, to sew, and to cook over an open fire.

My mother taught us bed making and clothes washing, and Marmie Jolivette's father, Carl, was always on hand to help with carpentry or any enterprise requiring a man's touch.

Miss Marian and Girl Scout troop—Below: Virginia Babson, me, Gladys Scott, Geri Payne, Betty Jane White, Carnie White, Marmie Jolivette, ____, Helen Hill, ____, ____, Gertrude Harrington, & Eleanor Cushman, Assistant Leader.

The official Scout magazine, "The American Girl," was my Bible and I devoured it each month. I remember one article that said a clean face was essential to good health, and a vigorous scrubbing each night would prevent wrinkles in old age. I have done it and am sorry to say that it hasn't worked, but it is the only advice that didn't serve me well.

Girl Scout troop in front of the library

CHAPTER 11
Teenage Years

As I started high school, I found there were many changes and new faces in our school. Elinor Nolan was a newcomer in the class ahead of me. Arlene Sanborn, Barbara Shepard, and my second cousin, Charlotte Galusha were new members of my class. Henry Cushman, who had been with us from first grade, had left for prep school. Our class was still small, with only twenty-eight in our graduating class. Most schools were similar to ours, having grades from kindergarten through high school. Consequently, our social activities included friends in school who were older and some who were younger.

Barbara Shepard, Elinor Nolan, Arlene Sanborn, and I soon became a foursome. We skated, skied, and swam together. We had overnights at each other's houses, talked about boys, and even learned to play poker. Arlene's father, who said this should be a part of every girl's education, taught our after-school poker classes. Poker was still considered a game played by men in a smoky poolroom, so it was a hard sell to our parents, but we loved it. And Mr. Sanborn was right.

One night we planned to go ice-skating at the pond. At the last minute, Elinor had to stay home to babysit for her little brother. We finally gave up trying to find a way for her to join us. It was a warm, late-winter night, and though the ice was hard, it was beginning to turn " rubbery" around the edges. On our way home, we took a shortcut near a sluiceway where the water under the ice was moving very fast. The ice under our feet slowly started to sink. We thrashed around, grabbing each other and the sinking ice, and at last we got to shore. We were completely soaked, glad to be alive, but worried about telling our parents. So, our friend Elinor came to our rescue. We stopped at her house, stripped off our wet clothes and dried them on the wood stove before going home. I often wonder why we were allowed to skate at night.

Elinor Nolan, Eileen Harte, and me

Dating was usually with a group of couples. Going on a date with only one boy was pretty serious business and not much fun. So, depending on how big the car was, at least two couples went to the movies or dancing at Hedges Lake or we just "drove around"—the equivalent of "hanging out." One summer, four of us drove out towards Petersburg to a tumbled-down house that we were sure was haunted. We laughed and necked—which only meant wrapping arms around each other's necks. We were young and so naive, and not really concerned about sex—well, maybe the boys were. However, none of us got pregnant because our mothers warned us never to kiss a boy! Did we? Oh, yes, occasionally, but with much fear and trepidation. What a thrill!

Most every weekend we went to the movies. They had improved since the days of *Rin-Tin-Tin* in Bank Hall. Now we went by bus to the General Stark or the Uptown Theater in Bennington, and though we went primarily to catch the latest episode of the weekly thriller, we knew every movie star in the films. We adorned our bedrooms with their pictures. In my room I had large blown up pictures of Clark Gable, Myrna Loy, Greta Garbo, Henry Fonda, and Carol Lombard. But the biggest treats were trips to Troy to the Roxy Theatre to see Gone With The Wind and The Wizard of Oz.

When I was about fifteen, I met Richie Fonteneau. He was sixteen, very handsome, and lived in Bennington. When he asked me to go to a dance at Bennington High School, I nearly fainted. He sent me a corsage that night with a card that said, "In sympathy." I still have it. We had fun together—we laughed a lot, went horseback riding, swimming at Lake Paran, and we danced—at Hedges Lake, at the Merry-go-round in Hoosick Falls, at Lake Bomoseen where Tommy Dorsey was playing or wherever a Big Band was playing We had many long talks on our front porch about what we wanted from life until Mother stopped us because the neighbors might "talk." We were very special friends.

The War in Europe was beginning to influence our lives. In the winter of 1938-39, Ritchie, Spike Freitag, and others of our friends joined the National Guard. They met once a month and went to training camp for two weeks in the summer. It seemed very romantic and noble, but how funny they looked in the old WWI uniforms. They were paid $15 a month, really enjoyed their training camp, and, of course, we didn't think they would ever go to "real" war.

Sixteen

CHAPTER 12
The Summer of '39

 The summer of 1939 when I was sixteen, my friend Elinor and I found summer jobs waiting on tables at the Barrows House in Dorset. We had taken a hotel course at school given by the Vermont Hotel Association and we felt qualified to run the whole place. But before we applied, our mothers went to Dorset and interviewed the Barrows to make sure they were okay. This did not make for very good relations between my mother and Mrs. Barrows, but we got the jobs—ten dollars a week, tips, and a place to live.

 We soon met Bill Barrows, Jr. and his friends, Porge West, Tim Gilbert, and Don Harwood. They were all college sophomores, and I later learned that they were assigned to keep us entertained. The Barrows were fearful we might get homesick and leave in the middle of the summer.

 With our new "worldly" friends, we listened to war news and tried to understand what was happening in Europe. When Hitler marched through Austria that summer, we listened to Edward R. Murrow and other commentators on the radio. We were concerned but couldn't believe the war could come to Vermont.

 It was worrisome, but we were young, and it was a wonderful summer. We worked hard and played hard. It was a new environment, we were on our own, and there were lots of things to do. The quarry "swimming pool" in South Dorset was the "hang out" when we weren't working and Elinor and I both loved to swim. Meals at the Barrows House were served from seven to nine in the morning, noon to two in the afternoon, and six-thirty to nine at night. During the day we made butter balls and salads, cleaned the refrigerators, arranged flowers, and relieved Bill, Jr. at the front desk. We had two hours "off" in the afternoon. Many nights we were so exhausted we just fell into bed. Our feet were killing us and when Don Harwood, a pre-med student, volunteered to come to our little house, the "Knit," and massage our feet, we were thrilled. It was considered okay because he was a "doctor!"

Two of the "Worldly Ones"
Tim Gilbert on left, Bill Barrows on right

However, we saved ourselves for Saturday night at the Equinox House. It was so glamorous and the string orchestra playing waltzes in the dining room was very romantic—a far cry from Hedges Lake! We drank Cokes and talked about the war and felt very sophisticated. I kept a diary.

One evening after work, Bill Barrows said to us, "The boys are going up to Red Garrett's house for a beer. Do you want to come?" Of course we did—we had heard about Red's mother and stepfather, Mr. Barber. They were the gossip of Dorset; the story of the Barber divorce and their au courant lifestyle had been the subject of a short story by Sally Benson in the New Yorker magazine. Being worldly these days, I, of course, had read the story. However, I wasn't prepared for the real thing. When we walked in the door, the boys were completely at ease. The walls of the room we entered were painted a dark turquoise and the floors were carpeted in white fur six inches deep.

Red's mother swooped into the room and greeted all the boys by name. They chatted comfortably with her, but I stood transfixed like an idiot. She truly was a sideshow girl, and I could imagine drums beating and music screeching as she stepped onstage. She was tall, had lots of bright red hair, was dressed in a long flowing gown and wonder of wonders, on her shoulder sat a monkey dressed in a diaper. Holy smoke, my grandmother will never believe this one! I thought.

Junior Prom 1941

CHAPTER 13

War

When the 40's began, we didn't realize there would be so very many changes in our lives. I began my senior year in high school in the fall of 1940. Many of my friends were graduated and on their way to college. I missed them, but they came home often. I was busy and my social life was a whirlwind.

Our drama club did Phillip Barrie's Holiday, and I played the part done by Katherine Hepburn. When someone sent me a corsage with a note "from an admirer," I was certain Broadway was my next stop. There were glee club concerts, field hockey games (I played forward on the team), gym exhibitions, junior proms, and senior balls in both Bennington and North Bennington. Skip Wright, from Bennington, invited me to go to Winter Carnival at Dartmouth; Steve Rainsford, a sophomore at Williams, took me to football games; and Bill Barrows asked me to come to the Fancy Dress Ball at Washington and Lee.

Underlying it all, though, was worry of the continuing war in Europe. Larry Powers occasionally stopped by our house and always prefaced the conversation by "Hi, Chub! What do you think of the European situation?" With that, my father started off on his analysis and predictions. The war was getting to be more than talk and was actually influencing our lives. In the fall of 1940, the Vermont National Guard was called to duty; this included Richie Fonteneau and Spike Freitag. We couldn't believe it! The special train carrying them all to Fort Devan stopped at the station in North Bennington. School was dismissed to allow us all to bid them goodbye. It was such a sad day. I kissed Richie goodbye, and we waved until the train was out of sight. After Fort Devan, he went to Flight Training School and became the captain of a B-24.

Richie Fonteneau—front row, right end, & B-24 crew

He was wounded while on a bombing run over Germany, taken prisoner, and toward the end of the war was released by Russian troops.

My high school class graduated in June of 1940, and I was accepted at Mary Washington College in Fredericksburg, Virginia. The tuition was $200 (it must have been for a semester). I went to the bank in fear and trembling. Mr. Ralph Jones—we had secretly nicknamed him Tiger—was the banker, and without hesitation he gave me the money. Whew, I was on my way!

In September, wearing my new shoes that hurt, I arrived in Fredericksburg to be greeted by Bill Barrows, who had come over from his school in Lexington. It was good to see a familiar face. I was assigned three roommates, Carleen Willoughby, Anita Devers, and Katie Herald, all from Virginia. We had a large room in Frances Willard Hall, and we soon knew everything about each other. I think they considered me sort of "fast" since Bill and my other friends had shown up so soon. In fact, scarcely a weekend went by without a visit from Bill.

I was taking a secretarial course that included shorthand (a supposedly short way of taking dictation using symbols for whole words), typing, bookkeeping, précis writing, and history (Civil War from the southern viewpoint, of course).

The rules were strict by today's standards. We could entertain boys only in the sitting room on the first floor; to leave the dorm on a weekend, we had to sign-out (even to go for a walk); and to leave the campus, we had to have written permission from our parents. Written permission from our parents meant waiting on the U.S. mail. This was the norm in most schools and didn't seem to be a hardship.

But one memorable Sunday, I came close to being expelled. Sadly, mass confusion and hysteria saved me. Bill Barrows had called to say he was coming over on Sunday morning with two other fraternity brothers. Could I find two dates for the boys? And he asked if we'd like to drive to Washington. A new shop called Dunkin' Doughnuts had just opened; we could try it and be back at school by four o'clock. I didn't give it a second thought. We checked out of the dorm and didn't think anyone would know that we didn't have permission to leave campus. Washington was very quiet that day and we assumed everyone was in church. Dunkin' Doughnuts was fabulous with so many variations on the original doughnut.

We arrived back on campus and as I walked into Willard Hall, trying to be as inconspicuous as possible, I was met by Anita Devers, who said, "Where have you been? We've been covering for you all day. Our Navy has been bombed at Pearl Harbor!" The dorm was in chaos. Many girls had boyfriends, brothers, uncles, cousins, and even fathers on those ships. We were without any further word on what had happened to them and there was a long line of weeping girls at the one telephone booth, trying to contact families. The dorm "mother" was fruitlessly trying to console and give advice to thirty girls. Everyone was crying.

News was slow in reaching us. Each day we listened to the one radio and poured over newspapers. Rumors were flying and attacks on the US west coast seemed probable. It was frightening and we all felt that if we could go home, we could deal with the situation. I worried that Art and Al might be drafted—but surely not my brother. He was too young. How wrong I was—ultimately they all were drafted.

We left two weeks later for the Christmas holidays. It was good to be home; nothing had changed and it felt secure. Nanny, having lived through the Civil War, the Spanish –American War, and WWI, was philosophical and calming as she got out her knitting needles once again for the troops. When we all gathered for Christmas at 42 Main Street, it was reassuring to be together.

We returned to school in January a little more thoughtful, a little more concerned, and a lot more responsible. We had grown up and faced the fact that our country and our wonderful way of life were being threatened. We were the generation that had to fight to preserve it. The thought was very sobering. There would be many bad days ahead, and we would lose many friends in the struggle. But to quote our president, Mr. Roosevelt, "With our abounding determination, we will gain the insurmountable triumph"—and we did.

There was an irony, however. This tremendous war effort by America and her allies would produce a spectacular leap forward in technology in all areas of our lives. Every aspect of science, medicine, education, transportation, entertainment, and even housekeeping would no longer be done "the old-fashioned way." In saving the world, as we had known it, we would be propelled, like our rockets on the fourth of July, into the fast moving high tech twenty-first century.

Acknowledgements

Most of all I want to thank my husband, Dick Williams. Throughout the writing and talking about this memoir, he has been most patient and even has been known to put his newspaper down, listen to my ramblings, and offer sage advice.

It took a lot of talk and memory-provoking to relive those days of seventy-five years ago, but with the help of my brother Frederick Simmons and two cousins Allen and Arthur Simmons, it all came back. However, it would have been a mad jumble without the expertise of my editor, Cheryl Lopanik, who encouraged me patiently for five years, kept me on track, typed and retyped, and brought some sort of order to the unrelated incidents.

Graphic designer Cyndi Follrich amazed me with her artistic ability. I am very grateful to her; she expertly scanned pictures in the story, retouched damaged photos, offered suggestions, and literally put life in the manuscript.

A special thanks goes to my oldest granddaughter Kirsten Wood, who started me on this path of reminiscences, and to grandson David Macquart-Moulin, whose only comment on reading about my early romances, said, "Oh, c'mon, Gran!" And I did tone it down a bit, David.